LAW AND JUSTICE IN CONTEMPORARY YEMEN

The People's Democratic Republic of Yemen
and
The Yemen Arab Republic

Other books by S. H. Amin

Middle East Legal Systems
Islamic Law in the Contemporary World
Marine Pollution in International and Middle Eastern Law
Remedies for breach of Contract in Islamic and Iranian Law
Wrongful Appropriation and Its Remedies in Islamic Law
Islamic Banking and Finance: The Experience of Iran
International and Legal Problems of the Gulf
Political & Strategic Issues in the Gulf
Iran-Iraq War: Legal Implications
Trading With Iran: Post-Revolution Law and Practice
Commercial Law of Iran
Basic Documents in Iranian Law
Legal and Political Structure of an
Islamic State: Implications for Iran and Pakistan
The Reason
(Commentaries on a Classic Text on Islamic Philosophy
according to Mulla Sadra Shirazi)
Islamic Law in Public and Business Context

LAW AND JUSTICE IN CONTEMPORARY YEMEN

The People's Democratic Republic of Yemen
and
The Yemen Arab Republic

by

S. H. AMIN

LL.B., LL.M., Ph.D., FIA
Reader/Associate Professor in Law at
Glasgow College of Technology

Glasgow:
ROYSTON LIMITED
1987

First published in 1987 by
ROYSTON LIMITED
10 Crown Road North
Glasgow G12 9DH
United Kingdom

British Library Cataloguing in Publication Data

Amin, S.H.
  Law and justice in contemporary Yemen:
  People's Democratic Republic of Yemen and
  Yemen Arab Republic.
  1. Law – Yemen
  I. Title
  345.3'3 (LAW)

  ISBN 0-946706-36-0

Printed in Great Britain by Bell and Bain Ltd., Glasgow

CONTENTS

FOREWORD

by: The Rt. Hon. Lord Campbell of Alloway,
One of Her Majesty's Counsel

This work on law and justice as applicable today in the Yemens is the latest of a long line of authoritative contributions by this distinguished author on Islamic law as applied to various legal systems in the Middle East. As in other Islamic legal systems, the fundamental source of law both in North and South Yemen rests upon the teachings of the Prophet as interpreted by Imams whose authority in this regard is acknowledged and respected. But notwithstanding differences in interpretation, the relationship between law, custom, tradition and theology is so close and so direct as to have become indestructable.

Both North and South Yemen constitutions acknowledge the supremacy of Islamic law as a State religion and as a source of law - subject to statutory provisions in certain areas of incidence. The perceived purpose of the law, however, differs as between North and South. In the North the conceptual approach is that the law should serve the interests of a free market economy: in the South the interests of a collective, institutionalised political and economic order as developed by popular participation.

This book is a serious definitive legal study and a valuable work of reference. But it is far more than that. It offers an informed exposition of the history, traditions and economies of the Yemens. Maps embellish the geographical narrative. Diagrams enhance the fiscal aspect. It is one of the most interesting, enjoyable and unusual law books that I have ever read: perhaps because it is so readable. Who would imagine that an accused tribesman to be tried by the Sultan is summoned by a thread from the fringe of the Sultan's kilt and may only obtain bail by the surrender of his dagger?

The work is well put together with a good table of contents, an index and a most useful bibliography. The author is to be congratulated. His labours are worthy of high commendation. A new dimension of law has been expounded with ease of style and clarity of expression.

Campbell of Alloway

House of Lords
29 January 1987

In preparing this book I have been assisted in different ways by a great number of institutions, colleagues and friends. The full list of all those institutions and individuals who have been generous with their help and support would be too long to record here. I should, first of all, mention those who acted as catalysts to my interest in contemporary Yemen. My old friend Noel Coulson (the late Professor of Islamic law in the School of Oriental and African Studies, London) was the first to raise my curiosity as to the stark contrast between the Yemen Arab Republic, as a Shi'a-dominated country, with Iran, another Shi'a-dominated society. We discussed and compared these two countries frequently after the Iranian revolution of 1979 in the context of a number of legal disputes in which we had been jointly retained as experts in Islamic law. This was what first stimulated my interest in modern Yemen. A year or two later Professor Kenneth Redden (University of Virginia) invited me to contribute a chapter on the legal system of south Yemen for *The Modern Legal System Cyclopedia* of which he was the general editor. I began researching the laws of post-independence South Yemen upon that invitation.[1]   Since then I have been fascinated by what is happening in the two Yemens. To both Professors Coulson and Redden I owe special thanks as my sources of inspiration.

Also acknowledge and gratitude go to many of my colleagues at the Glasgow College for their counsel, co-operation, encouragement and support. My research assistants and postgraduate students were full of enthusiasm, although none was prepared to write a project on the oil-poor contemporary Yemen. The College library staff were, as usual, of tremendous help. Another colleague, Michael Quinn, provided me with original photographs and enlightening memories of his experience as a British soldier in Aden and Southern Arabia. To all these colleagues I express my sincere thanks.

I am also indebted to many colleagues and friends from outside my own college who have facilitated my research endeavours over the past few years. Dean John P. Grant (Dean of the Glasgow University Law School), has been a great source of support and encouragement, particularly in the early stages of my research. My learned brother, Sayed Muhammad Amin (Theological College, Qum, Iran) proved a tremendous intellectual support and advised on doctrinal and theological aspects of the Zaidi branch of Shi'ism. Professor Tahir Mahmood (Professor of Islamic Law, University of Delhi, India), Professor Tourkhan Orfi Gandjei (Professor of Persian and Turkish in the

---

1 . My contribution was published in the fifth volume of the *Modern Legal Systems Cyclopedia*, Buffalo, New York: William S. Hein, 1985. My contribution to South Yemeni law also includes an article written in English but published in a German periodical i.e. *Hannoversche Studien Uber den Mittleren Osten*, Band 1 (1986), pp. 56-57.

University of London), Professor Hamid Mowlana (American University, Washington D.C.) and Professor Syed Ali Ashraf (President of the Islamic Academy, Cambridge,England) have been generous with their time and have all helped me in different ways. Amongst numerous professional colleagues Mr. Peter J.E. Jackson (Barrister and Crown Court Recorder, London) deserves special acknowledgement. Through Peter Jackson I established many useful contacts which included a number of British and European firms which had interests in this part of the Middle East. Finally, I must take this opportunity also to thank my wife, Elspeth, without whose help and care this book could not have been written.

S. H. AMIN

Department of Law
Glasgow Institute of Technology
Cowcaddens Road
Glasgow G4 OBA
Telephone: 041-332 7090
Telex: 779341

PREFACE

This book is intended to present a short exposition of law and justice in contemporary Yemen, covering both the People's Democratic Republic of Yemen, PDRY (South Yemen) and the Yemen Arab Republic, YAR (North Yemen). The two Yemens have adhered to two totally opposed principles for their political, constitutional and legal evolution. They are also pursuing two fundamentally distinctive policies for their respective economic development and social reform. Laying claims to contemporaneity, this volume deals with the main current problems pertaining to the constitional regimes, legal and administrative systems, and social, political and economic structures of South and North Yemen.

The contrast between the political, legal and economic systems of South and North Yemen, as they stand today, is very sharp. South Yemen is an ultra-radical hard-line Communist State while North Yemen is a moderate nationalist State. South Yemen is in a 'strategic alliance' with the Soviet Union while North Yemen is a constituent part of the world capitalist system. South Yemen follows a rigid Marxist-Leninist ideology while North Yemen follows modernist reformist policies without any identifiable ideological basis. South Yemen is extremelly biased towards the Communist world but North Yemen is willing to trade with any country and accept foreign aid wherever offered. Hence North Yemen maintains diplomatic and trade relations with both the United States and Soviet Union, although it is undeniably more influenced by the interests of the free market economy. South Yemen attempts to detribalise and 'democratise' its population mainly by force of ideological inspiration, Marxist indoctrination, political education and socialist culture. North Yemen, committed to the pusuit of economic development, wishes to catch up with the modern world by rapid economic growth, legal reforms, Westernisation, industrialisation and urbanisation. These different international and domestic policies obviously have different ramifications for all aspects of political, economic and legal life.

This book is composed of a preface and four substantive chapters. Chapter 1, as an introduction, provides the basic data pertaining to the geographical dimensions, political environment and economic structure of contemporary Yemen. Chapter 2 and 3 outline the general patterns of law and justice in South and North Yemen respectively. Each chapter deals with the constitutional regime, form of government and public administration, legal history, sources of law, development of the national legal systems, judiciary, legal education and legal profession of each country. These chapters also deal with selective areas of substantive and procedural law including crime and punishment, family relations, agriculture and fisheries, law of the sea, commerce, foreign trade, banking, insurance and provision of social services. The emphasis throughout is upon a discussion of general principles and basic patterns, rather than a capitulation of details. Having described the basic trends of legal development in the three previous chapters, Chapter 4, in the form of a conclusion, offers an analytical study of the various legal issues covered in the previous chapters. This concluding chapter is intended to analyse, explain, discuss, compare and contrast all the striking differences in substance between South and North Yemen.

To date, there has been no single book published in any European language on law and justice in contemporary Yemen.[1] This may be a reflection of the fact North and South Yemen are amongst the poorest nations in the world. Unlike their neighbouring oil-rich Arab countries, the two Yemen are oil - poor. So the Yemens are neglected while their immediate neighbours e.g. Saudia Arabia attract the attention of the world's business and political communities. In a world dominated by monetary considerations, one may not expect the Western market to demand much information on the operation of law in impoverished contemporary Yemen. This present contribution is the first to appear as a full-length book on this most interesting, but neglected, topic.[2]

I may add that I anticipate that the world will hear more and more of the two Yemens in the forseeable future. On the one hand, North Yemen will soon be an oil-exporting State, and a member of OPEC, so it will inevitably attract greater attention from the rest of the world, in the same way that other oil-rich Arab countries have become a centre of attention. We may soon witness a rush of Western businessmen and their advisors to San'a to negotiate deals for all sorts of trade and projects ranging from selling consumer goods to bidding for major construction contracts and infrastructure projects. The People's Democratic Republic of Yemen too will be more in the news because of its strategic significance and politcal militancy. The Democratic

1. This is not intended to diminish the value of efforts made to date by various writers, researchers and scholars to study Yemeni law. For a full list of these relevant contributions see the bibliography section at the end of this book, pp. 129-140.

2. A couple of unpublished doctoral dissertations and several essays and booklets are the only literature on legal developments in contemporary Yemen so far produced. Amongst doctoral theses references should be made to KAZI, A.K. *al-Muntakhab fi al-Fiqh lil Hadi, London,* 1958, MAKTARI, A.M.A., *Water Rights and Irrigation Practices in Lahij,* Cambridge, 1971 and ZEIN AL-ABDIN, T., *The Role of Islam in the State,* Cambridge, 1975. On South Yemen a thin pamphlet has been published by Islam Ghanem entitled *Yemen: Political History, Social Structure and Legal Systems,* London 1981. On North Yemen a well researched typewritten pamphlet has been produced by Yorguy Hakim entitled *Yemen Arab Republic: A Country Law Study,* Washington DC, 1985.

Yemen controls the Strait of Bab al-Mandab and claims a 200 mile jurisdictional zone in the Red Sea, the Gulf of Aden, the Arabian Sea and the Indian Ocean.[3]

The Democratic Yemen's maritime position on the strategic Strait of Bab al-Mandab, which separates the Red Sea from the Indian Ocean, is the same as that of Iran's position on the Strait of Hormuz and the Persian-Arabian Gulf. The Strait of Bab-al Mandab falls within the territorial seas of the People's Democratic Republic of Yemen and the Republic of Djibouti.

By Article 38 of the United Nations Convention on the Law of the Sea 1982, all ships and aircraft enjoy the right of "transit passage" in and over international straits. The Straits of Bab al-Mandab too is international in character in the sense that it is used for international navigation. Thus in spite of the fact that its waters fall within the limits of the territorial seas of South Yemen and Djibouti, these coastal States may not impede the freedom of navigation and overflight. While international navigation may not be impeded, South Yemen and Djibouti have the right to (a) regulate maritime traffic, (b) enforce their anti-pollution laws, and (c) enforce their fiscal, immigration and sanitary laws. This jurisdiction must be applied in a universal and indescriminate fashion. In short, while South Yemen cannot impede navigation and overflight, it can lawfully arrest any ship suspected of breaching its law and regulations.[4]

The control of these extensive maritime zones by South Yemen is a matter of concern to the free world because of this country's alignment with the Soviet Union. The situation is made more acute by the fact that South Yemen's land and sea boundaries, particularly those with North Yemen and Oman, are unsettled. These onshore and offshore boundary disputes are additional potential sources armed conflict and war in an already tense and volatile region. Formally, only a partial border exists between North Yemen and South Yemen, drawn by the British and the Ottoman Empires in 1905. The South Yemen-Oman border is also undefined. There is a possibility that Oman may be de-stabilised by the activities of Communist guerillas in the Dhofar region supported by South Yemen, the Soviets and Cubans. This could seriously interfere with the supply of oil to the West and Japan. Also, in the event of any Communist advances in Dhofar, all the smaller conservative governments of the Gulf region would be threatened.

3. The text of the appropriate legislation on maritime zones claimed by the People's Democratic Republic of Yemen has been reproduced as Appendix 2 at the end of this book. See infra pp. 117-125.

4. For a legal discussion of the regime of international straits see AMIN, S.H. "The regime of international straits: legal implications for the Strait of Hormuz", 12 *Journal of Maritime Law and Commerce* (1981) pp. 387-405.

Aden attained its independence from Great Britain through armed struggle in the 1960's, and the Democratic Yemen of today takes pride in this radical tradition which actually forced the British to leave Aden in total desperation. The experience of the British Empire in Aden and Southern Arabia was unique in that it was given no opportunity to hand over power to the post-colonial government. The National Liberatin Front (NLF) having driven the British out, took power in South Yemen in its own right. The anti-colonial struggle led to the establishment of an ultra-radical, revolutionary and militant People's Democratic Republic which identified closely with the Communist world. The PDRY is the only Communist State in the Arab world based on a radical Marxist model.

The Soviet Union has patiently invested time and energy in the Democratic Yemen's military forces, economy and government over the past twenty years. One day the Soviets may decide to intervene more directly in Southern Arabia and/or the Horn of Africa. In that case, the Soviet Union would make use of the strategic positions of its client States such as the PDRY and Ethiopia. Under the terms of the USSR-PDRY Treaty of Friendship and Co-operation of 1979, the Soviet Union and the PDRY are to 'co-operate' in the military field. The word 'co-operation' is totally inappropriate. The Democratic Yemen is a simple recipient of military aid and could not 'co-operate' with the sophisticated military might of the Soviet Union. All it can do in terms of co-operation is to provide military bases and facilities on its mainland and outlaying island territories for the use of the Soviet Union. The Soviet Union, to say the very least, wishes to restrict Western influence on the Arabian Peninsula and the Democratic Yemen may well prove to be the most effectual instrument for achieving that objectice.[5]

Tne legal system of the Democratic Yemen is projected as a socialist legal system in the areas of constitutional, administrative and public law. Drawing on Marxist - Leninism, "democratic centralism" and "scientific socialism" as interpreted by the Soviet Union, the Democratic Yemen is committed to 'detribalisation' and 'democratization'. The Constitution prescribes universal suffrage in the election of assemblies and councils of national and local government. More importantly, both in law and practice, the Yemeni Socialist Party has a leading role, exercising full control over the society and State according to the Leninist principle of 'democratic centralisra'. This

---

5. See AMJN, S.H., *Political and Strategic Issues in the Gulf*, Glasgow: Royston, 1984, pp. 39-41. For a more up to date account of Soviet policies in the PDRY and its neighbouring countries see KATZ, M.N., *Russia and Arabia: Soviet Foriegn Policy toward the Arabian Peninsula*, John Hopkins University Press, 1986. Also see LACKNER, H., *P.D.R. Yemen: Outpast of Socialist Development*, London, Ithaco Press, 1985.

ruling Communist Party has the absolute power to determine policy and all the organs of State must follow and execute the will of the Party. Thus the formal structures of government and constitutional order are comparatively irrelevant and practically of little consequence. In areas of private law, particularly those concerned with family relations and personal status, the South Yemeni law is still based on the one hand on Islamic law and on the other on traditional customary and tribal norms.

While the application of Islamic law is dominant in urbanised Aden, the customary law is the norm amongst the tribesmen. Outside Aden, the population is still largely made up of tribespeople who live in an around villages or settlements. These tribes group together in a number of tribal confedarations. Each confederation applies its own customary law and standards as administered by tribal arbitrators. The Marxist regime of Aden strongly disapproves of such fragmentation of the nation into tribal units. The State is committed to develop a pan-tribal legal system to be applied universally nationwide. Detribalisation is considered as essential for the creation of a national character. Thus the ruling party is committed to push aside all aspects of customary law and traditional norms in favour of socialist measures.

As befits a Communist State, all the basic means of production distribution and exchange in the PDRY are under public ownership. The government has a rigid policy of forced collectivisation. It exercises a monopoly over all the viable economic sectors and strictly supervises all other areas of economic activity. Private enterprise is restricted and treated with suspicion, the State assuming full overall responsibility for all aspects of trade and industry. The Democratic Yemen is creating new institutions, legal frameworks, political patterns and social, cultural and educational standards to transform itself into a pan-tribal socialist State. It is significant that South Yemen has opted to create a secular socialist system, as opposed to building up an 'Islamic socialist" State as advocated by Qadhdhafi in Libya as well as by other activists in a number of Muslim countries.

The Yemen Arab Republic, North Yemen, in contrast with South Yemen, is attempting to bring its political, economic and legal systems in line with the modern world i.e. the capitalist industrialised countries. It aspires to join the ranks of moderate developing countries by following modernist-reformist policies. It is developing its national institutions and legal system on the basis of political neutrality, secularism, anti-Communism, free enterprise and open-door economic policies. These principles were embodied in the Permanent Constitution of 1970 which represented the views of the moderate republicans as well as those of the moderate monarchists.[6]

6. During the period 1962-1970, the royalists fought a counter-revolution and were backed by Saudia Arabia. For almost a decade, the republicans failed to establish unquestionable supremacy over the entire Yemeni territory.

The revolutionary republicans, having become reconciled with the monarchists, have since the early 1970's followed a systematic plan for building up the country's infrastructure and economic development. The constitutional and legal principles are aimed at political and social cohesion without disturbing traditional forms. The 1970 Constitution which has been suspended in 1974 was eventually reinstated by the most recent constitutional document promulgated in August, 1982 in the form of a National Charter.[7] No-one can deny that North Yemen has grown out of its isolationist and inward looking attitude which was the norm under the Imams. But it is also undeniable that economic development requires political development. The post-Imamate YAR has achieved neither to date.

The reinstatement in 1982 of the Constitution, in itself a signal of political stabiliity, may provide an opportunity for further political and economic development in North Yemen. A National Charter promulgated in August 1982 clarified the political and economic policies of the YAR. It declared North Yemen's support for an open economy and free trade. The National Charter also guaranteed a number of civil and economic rights, including equal opportunity, social justice and respect for private property. It should be noted, however, that many such public proclamations ar eintended to counter the charges made by the anit-government opposition National Democratic Front (NDF) who are supported by South Yemen and Libya. In North Yemen the creation of a modern and secular legal system, based on relatively liberal economic ideas and free trade, is part of this country's attempt at economic development. The YAR already provides a favourable environment for domestic and foreign investment.[8]

Agriculture is still the mainstay of the North Yemeni economy, providing 70 per cent of the GNP and 90 per cent of all exports. Until now, however, North Yemen's major foreign exchange earners have been foreign aid and the remittances of the Yemeni labour force working all over the world (including in such unexpected places as Newcastle-Upon-Tyne in England and Detroit, USA). This situation may well change once the exploitation of North Yemen's oil and gas resources brings real revenue to the public treasury. The Yemen Oil and Minerals Corporation (YOMINCO), established in 1978, is the State instrumentality responsible for the exploration and exploitation of minerals, including particularly oil and gas resources. The promising discoveries by Hunt Oil in 1984-85 are expected to be exploited by 1989. This will generate additional revenue for the government and

7. The issuance of a 'National Charter' or 'Bill of Rights' as a constitutional document is a familiar practice in the Arab world. Gamal Abdel Nasser issued the first National Charter in Egypt in 1962. Algeria promulgated another National Charter in 1976. For details, see ABU BAKR FATTAH, *Politics and Government in Algeria*, Glasgow: Royston, 1987.

8. See Chapter 3, pp. 73-78 and Chapter 4, pp. 88-89 and 98-100.

will create an unparalleled boost to the public sector economy. One can then expect a far keener interest in North Yemen by the business community in the free market economies, particularly the oil consuming West and Japan.

I have no doubt than once Yemeni oil finds its way into the international market, we shall see more literature on all aspects of the Yemen Arab Republic, including its legal and judicial system. Many North Yemenis hope that what happened in the Gulf States in the 1970's will be repeated in North Yemen in the 1990's. Almost a quarter of the total public expenditure in the Third Five-Year Plan (1987-1991) is allocated to the oil and gas exploration and exploitation programme. Another one fifth of the budget is set aside for infrastructure projects. The third largest item of expenditure (some fifteen per cent) is reserved for agriculture and industry.[9] This prioritasation in planning demonstrates that North Yemen's economy in the 1990's will be dominated by the oil and gas sector. In addition to the energy sector, there are other sectors of economy which will be of interest to foreign suppliers and investors e.g. the development of the infrastructure, light industry, agriculture, and exploitation of mineral resources which have not as yet been thoroghly surveyed.[10]

It seems clear that North Yemen is now one of the most committed of the Muslim States towards the pursuance of the ideal of a modernist reformist system of government in the course of speeding up its economic development. Having broken with its sacred and traditional system of governance under the Imams, North Yemen is now a secular State, following nationalist modernist tendencies. This is quite remarkable in an era when many Muslim nations have come to realise that the role of Islam in their political and legal process should be intensified.[11]

It should be noted that Islamic resurgence is more visible in those Muslim countries which have had a chance to experiment with secularist ideologies. The case of Iran was a clear example of this situation. The Shah (who died in exile in Egypt in July 1980) has pushed for complete secularisation, modernisation and Westernisation of Iran's military, administrative, legal, judicial, financial, educational, academic, cultural and economic structure. The Iranian revolution of 1979 was built on religious sentiments and a popular rejection of a secularist, Westernised and dictatorial regime supported by the World's

9. EL MALLAKH, R., *The Economic Development of the Yemen Arab Republic,* London: Croom Helm, 1986, at p. 182, based on estimation of Dr. Abdul Aziz SAQQAF, in April 1986.

10. The visit by Douglas Hurd, the British Minister of State in the Foreign and Commonwealth Office, to San'a in 1982 was a step in this direction.

11. For a good account of this position see NOORI, Y. and AMIN, S.H., *Legal and Political Structure of an Islamic State,* Glasgow: Royston, 1987.

political and economic order. This Iranian example serves to demonstrate that is is usually after excessive indulgence in one direction that a nation attempts to correct itself by using an antithetic system. History shows that there is a cyclical pattern of Islamic decline and Islamic reŝurgence.

It may be that North Yemen is still in its early secularist cycle. After all, for centuries Yemen was isolated from the rest of the world under the quast-theocratic system of Imamate. The Imams acted as both spiritual and temporal leaders of the community for centuries. The YAR's experience of secular republicanism goes back no more than twenty odd years. It is fair to say that the YAR perhaps has not yet fully matured as a completely secular modern State. Nor has North Yemeni society gone through the challenge and frustration that other oil-rich Muslim societies have experienced. Thus its enthusiasm for both secularism and oil wealth is understandable at this stage of its political and economic development.

As it will become apparent, this book has an inter-disciplinary and comparative nature. It will be of interest not only to those specialising in comparative law and Middle East/Islamic Studies, but also to a wider readership. Unlike many other writings on Middle Eastern and Islamic law published since the advent of oil, the scopé fo this study is not limited to the legal aspects affecting international trade and commerce in the two countries under review. Here we discuss not only the constitutional, administrative and commercial law which is directly relevant to business activities, but also many areas wich are not related to international commerce e.g. family law, personal status, women's rights, criminal law and the penal system. Indeed the author has made a special effort to compare the relative provisions for social justice and social services in the two Yemens. This emphasis is relfected in the title of this book which refers not only to the 'law' but also to 'justice' in contemporary Yemen.

Anyone interested in the operation and development of law in developing countries should find something of interest in this book, whether his or her main interest be law, politics, international relations, economics or development studies. This work, I hope, will be particularly useful from the point of view of comparing and contrasting the development (or under-development) of the law and public administration in the two Yemens. It should also be of interest from the point of interaction between law and socio-economic change. I have discussed these points in some detail in Chapter 4. So while the first three cahpters provide a basically descriptive study of legal and law related issues, the last chapter contains mainly an analytical discussion. The emphasis of this analytical and comparative study is pa|ced on the opposing systems of law and administration operating in North and South Yemen and the impact of these legal trends on the social and economic environment.

8

Chapter 1

THE CONTEMPORARY YEMEN

I GENERAL INTRODUCTION

The two Yemens (North and South) are situated in the south-west of the Arabian Peninsula. Throughout the history, both countries have formed a single area and have enjoyed long periods of peace and harmony, in spite of the fact that they were never totally united in the political sense. The present borders between the two Yemens were drawn up by the colonial powers, the Turks in the north, the British in the south, in the 20th century. These two countries together go under the name of the Yemen and are the subject of this book.

In this introductory section we shall attempt to provide some general background information about the geographical, political and economic aspects of the two Yemens. Then we shall proceed to discuss matters of law and justice which are the main object of this book.

II THE PEOPLE'S DEMOCRATIC REPUBLIC OF YEMEN

1. Factual Data

The People's Democratic Republic of Yemen, alternatively known as Democratic Yemen or South Yemen,[1] is located at the south-eastern part of the Arabian Peninsula. It is bounded by Saudi Arabia to the north, by Oman to the east, by the Arabian Sea and the Gulf of Aden to the south, and by North Yemen (Yemen Arab Republic) to the west. Comprising the former territory of Aden and 23 sheikhdoms, the Democratic Yemen has an area of 300,000 square kilometers approximately – making it much larger than the neighbouring North Yemen in terms of size. The country has a population of just less than two million. The inhabitants of the whole of this country are Shafi'i Sunni Muslims.[2]

1. The name adopted by the NLF in 1967 for the independent southern Yemen was People's Republic of South Yemen. The Constitution of November 1970 changed the name of the country to People's Democratic Republic of Yemen. This change of name reflected the thinking of the ruling party in two ways. First, the omission of the word south meant a commitment to to a united Yemen. Secondly, the addition of the word of Democratic meant a commitment to socialist ideology.

2. The Shafi'i school founded by Muhammad ibn Idris Shafi'i (767-821 AD) is the middle ground betwen the methodological school of Abu Hanifa (699-767 AD) and the traditionalist approach of the Malik ibn Anas (713-795 AD). For further details see AMIN S. H., *Islamic Law: Introduction, Glossary and Bibliography,* Glasgow, 1985, pp. 3-8.

2. Economic Structure

The Democratic Yemen is a 'socialist developing country.'[3] Its national economy is composed of three sectors (a) the State sector, (b) the private sector and (c) the mixed sector. The private sector has been largely diminishing as a result of the State's socialistic policies. The State sector, holding 76 per cent of the total national economy, is by far the most dominant sector in the national economy. The government ascribes to a rigidly centralist economy and collectivisation. The mixed sector (i.e. participation between the public and private sectors) produces some 16 per cent of industrial output.

The Democratic Yemen is one of the poorest countries in the world, with a per capita income of less than $500. It is recognised by the United Nations as one of the 20 least developed nations in the world. Trade regulations are stringent and closely supervised by the State. The country has a limited agriculture sector and a small industrial base. Until 1967 the economy had been sustained by the position of Aden as a shipping port. The Aden refineries (belonging to the B.P.) were also a source of industrial employment. After the independence, relative prosperity came to an end as a result of British and European withdrawal.

In Southern Arabia only a small proportion of land is fit for cultivation, and water resources are scarce. Nevertheless, only about a quarter of the country's cultivable land is used. The Democratic Yemen, therefore has a very underdeveloped system of agriculture. Agricultural output in 1979 was as low as 7.9 per cent of gross domestic product (GDP).

The absence of surveyed mineral deposits, poor links between different areas, inadequately developed telecommunication, and other geographical and social difficulties has hindered economic development. Large-scale geological survey projects and drillings in search of oil and gas resources have to date proved unsuccessful, although the oil explorations in the disputed territory between the two Yemens are promising.

The Democratic Yemen is heavily dependent on external aid flows for its survival. These loans and grants which are given by the oil-rich Arab countries, Europe, the Soviet Union, China and the International Monetary Fund account for as much as 70 per cent of

3. The term 'developing country' generally expresses a judgement about the stage of economic development reached by a particular country. However, socialist countries are generally not included in this category – regardless of their stage of development.

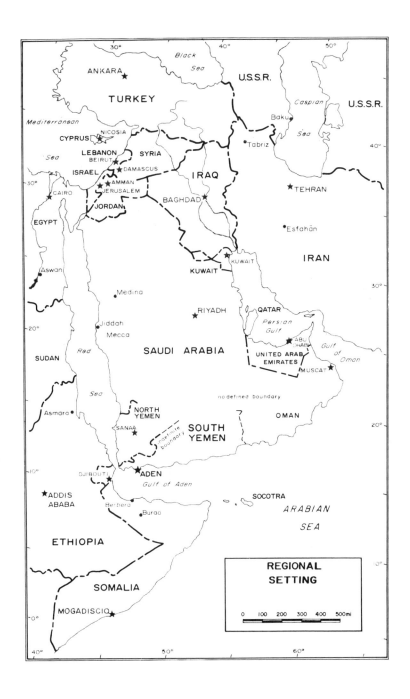

REGIONAL
SETTING

0   100   200   300   400   500mi

the national budget. The government disclosed during the first Five-Year Development Plan (1974-79) that only 22 per cent of the budget came from domestic sources. This may be the result of a policy of collectivisation, imposing a doctrinair economic system. The country's second Five-Year Development Plan (1981-85) called for resolute measures to mobilise domestic resources and to cut the budget deficit. The plan called for expenditures of $1.6 billion, allocating 29 per cent of the total expenditure to industry while 31 per cent of the total expenditure was allocated to socio-economic services.

The public sector is heavily dependent on foreign finance for its capital spending, as locally financed investment is negligible. Up until the late 1970's, nearly 70 per cent of all aid to South Yemen was from the socialist bloc, with the USSR contributing 40 per cent and China 16 per cent. Since 1970 the USSR has remained South Yemen's main development partner under a series of economic agreements, the latest of which was signed in mid 1982.

Worker's remittances and private transfers (estimated at $450 million in 1982) are the other main sources of external finance, accounting for up to about two thirds of all imports. The country has in recent years acquired large external debts (approximately equivalent to its GNP) in spite of the fact that much of the debts were given on concessional terms or in the form of grants. President Ali Naser Muhammad, who was in power during the 1980-86, attempted to tackle these economic problems by ending the country's hostile relations with the oil rich conservative Arab States thus attracting their financial assistance. However, a bloody struggle for power which ended in the Civil War of January 1986 did not allow for such attempts to come to fruition.

Conclusion

A low resource base, low levels of consumption, low productivity and a growing foreign trade deficit have created a weak economy, despite low salaries and high taxes. The country's balance of payments is characterised by a growing trade deficit, estimated at $730 mn for 1983, and a continued heavy dependence on foreign aid and workers' remittances. Debt servicing on the country's net foreign borrowings is fast becoming a heavy burden, rising from YD27.3 mn in 1980 to YD47.9 mn ($134 mn) in 1981. The per capita income is estimated at U.S. $500 which makes South Yemen the poorest nation in the Middle East.

The revised second five year plan (1981-85) planned for more than 200 projects in all sectors at a total cost of about $1,600 mn, of which 70 per cent ($1,120 mn) was provided by external assistance, with government resources providing the remainder. However, following the Civil War of January 1986, the oil rich conservative Arab States will be very reluctant to provide further financial aid to this country. The Civil War demonstrated that the leadership in South Yemen is not only hostile to neighbouring countries, but it is also incapable to settle their own internal differences without bloodshed and destruction. In the circumstances, only the Soviet Union may feel obliged to continue, or even increase, its financial grants and loans for reconstruction, in order to control further unrest in this faithful Marxist Arab State.

Foreign Relations

The Democratic Yemen has close ties with the USSR and the socialist world. To confirm this position, the Soviet Prime Minister Kosygin visited the Democratic Yemen in September 1979. When President Abd al-Fattah Isma'il of the Democratic Yemen visited the USSR in October 1979, a Treaty of Friendship and Co-operation was signed between the two countries. This treaty, which is to last 20 years, is reminiscent of similar Soviet treaties with Ethiopia, Angola, Mozambique and Afghanistan and in effect brings the Democratic Yemen firmly into Soviet camp.[4]

The Democratic Yemen also upholds the international political principles of the USSR. It contributed to the Soviet-Cuban effort in the Ogaden war. It signed an agreement in August 1981 with two other Soviet-backed regimes (Libya and Ethiopia) to counterbalance American efforts to establish a presence in the Gulf region and Arabia. It is also a member of the Steadfastness Front together with other Arab allies of the USSR.

President Ali Naser Muhammad, ousted during the civil war of January 1986, campaigned for moderate regional accommodation. He eventually restored diplomatic relations with Oman and even achieved a modicum of co-operative interaction with Saudi Arabia. After the civil war of January 1986, Haidar Abu Bakr al-Attas, the former Prime Minister under Ali Naser, was installed as President. The new regime has issued several statements trying to confirm its good neighbour commitments. The general view, however, remains that the Democratic Yemen will continue to insert its

4. For full accounts of this treaty see AMIN, S. H., *Political and Strategic Issues in the Gulf,* Glasgow: Royston, 1984, pp. 39-42.

The Yemens

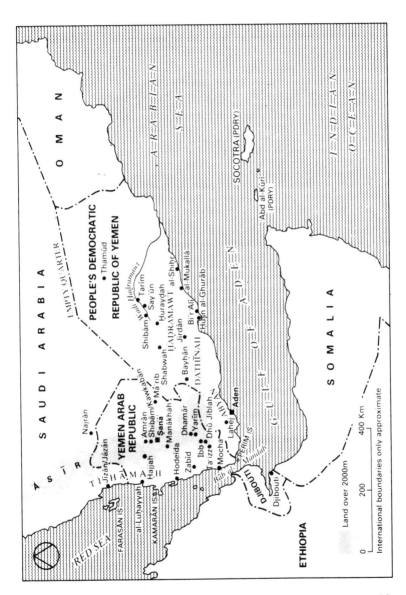

destabilising pressures against its conservative Arab neighbours as soon as its own internal circumstances permit such indulgences.

III THE YEMEN ARAB REPUBLIC

1. Factual Data

North Yemen, officially called the Yemen Arab Republic, is situated in the south-west of Saudi Arabia, bordering the Red Sea and the Strait of Bab al-Mandab. It occupies the area between Saudi Arabia and the People's Democratic Republic of Yemen.

The country has a population of nine million and an area of 195,000 sq. km. It is chiefly a mountainous country, with a high relief intensity. Save its urban trade centres along the frankincense route North Yemen is basically a rural society. This rural bias stands in contrast to the situation in South Yemen where the Aden Port has always been a major urban and commercial base. In North Yemen there is still a tribal peasantry, with a pronounced territorially defined tribal organisation. This socio-economic structure had contributed to the survival of the under-developed urban and trade communities. Since the early 1970's, however, the Government has pursued a policy of complete opening up to the world market and has thus embarked on rebuilding of the modern Yemen Arab Republic on a nationalist reformist pattern.

North Yemen's population is mostly Arab, more than half belonging to the Zaidite branch of Shi'a Islam, based in the north, and the rest belonging to the Shafi'i school of Sunni Islam, living in the south. Prior to the 1962 revolution, North Yemen maintained a very rigid social hierarchy. This traditional social order discriminated heavily against the majority of the population in favour of 'noble blood'. At the very top of the social classes were the ruling Sayeds (collectively called *Sada*) claiming direct descent from the Prophet Muhammad. Immediately after the Sayeds, were members of various tribes (*qabili* i.e. member of a qabila/tribe) considered also as having a decent and honourable ancestry. In such a situation, tribal allegiance played an important role in political and social bias. Lastly, in this birth-conscious society, the lower class consisted of all other people who were 'without descent'. Called *nuqqas*, the lower class were engaged in occupations which were despised by other members of the society. They were deprived of any sense of honour and social esteem: The republican regime soon abolished these discriminations when it

14

A yemeni wearing an indigo *qub'* turban, and over his *zinnah* a *qamīṣ* of the cloth called *Misrī* (with the sleeves tied up for work) and a *lihfah* shoulder-cloth wound round his *jambiyyah*. (Photo: Mundy, 1975.)

came to power in 1962. In practice, however, the old social order still remains more or less unchanged. This can be seen by observing the rate of illiteracy which is around 80 per cent and lack of social mobility in the contemporary North Yemen.

The social texture of North Yemen is not uniform. The main division originates from the conflict between customary practices and state-backed legal requirements. The old regime of the Imams consistently tried to establish the role of Shari'a (Islamic law) with a view to undermine the customary powers of the local and tribal chiefs. They failed to do so. It is in the same spirit more or less that the republican regime is now attempting to introduce a secular legal system that may be enforced throughout the whole country.

2. Economic Structure

North Yemen was virtually isolated from the outside world prior to 1962. This situation coupled with its dependence upon subsistence agriculture allowed North Yemen to become (on a per capita basis), one of the poorest third world countries. Since 1970, fairly rapid economic development has taken place,[5] and Yemen Arab Republic has shown a desire to encourage foreign participation in this expansion process. Nevertheless, this country's economy remains agricultural with more than 80 per cent of the population deriving their livelihood from the land. Wheat, coffee, barley and corn are the most common products of the country.

The Yemen Arab Republic suffers from persistent weakness in its balance of payments. Certain measures were introduced between 1983 and 1985 to restrain domestic spending and imports. These measures included wage restraint and reductions in development spending, together with a major revenue-mobilisation effort focussing on increases in tax and duty rates and on improvements in the tax collection mechanism. The application of these restraints resulted in significant budget deficit reductions in 1983 and 1984 – both in absolute terms and as proportions of GDP – despite the continuing decline in official budgetary support from neighbouring countries. The Government's tighter fiscal stance was reinforced by the actions of the Central Bank, which in 1984 doubled commercial bank reserve requirements to 20 per cent in an effort to absorb some

---

5. In early 1972 the Central Planning Organisation (an outgrowth of the existing Technical Office) was entrusted with economic development and planning for economic progress. The first economic development Plan came into force in 1974 and ever since the planning has continued. For details see *infra, pp. 18-19.*

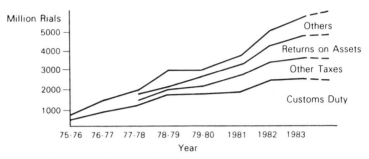

YAR: Government Revenue by Sectors

Sources: Ministry of Finance, *The Government Budget* and *Final Accounts Statistics* (San'a').

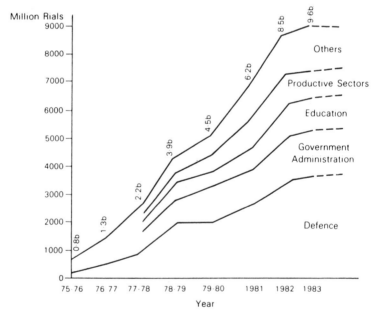

YAR: Government Expenditures by Sectors

Sources: Ministry of Finance, *The Government Budget* and *Final Accounts Statistics* (San'a').

of the excess liquidity in the banking system. Although such fiscal restraints has resulted in a degree of decline in the balance of payment deficit, North Yemen's economic prospects still remain under considerable pressure.*

Yemen Arab Republic: Balance of Payments

	1981	1982	1983	1984	Projected 1985
		(million U.S. dollars)			
Exports	11	5	10	9	10
Imports	-1,748	-1,952	-1,796	-1,414	-1,170
Services (net)	-52	-37	-52	-46	-70
Unrequited transfers (net)	1,125	1,393	1,293	1,137	990
OF WHICH:					
Government receipts	*337*	*469*	*189*	*143*	*120*
Private receipts	*988*	*1,191*	*1,244*	*1,067*	*960*
Current account	-664	-592	-545	-313	-240
Nonmonetary capital (net)	404	282	328	169	80
Overall balance	-260	-311	-216	-144	-160

Data: Yemen Arab Republic, Central Planning Organisation, Ministry of Finance, and Central Bank of Yemen; IMF staff estimates

Various Sectors of the Economy

The Yemen Arab Republic maintains three main economic sectors, namely: (a) public sector, (b) private sector and (c) mixed sector (joint ventures and participation between the private and public sectors). The public sector, so far as industry and commerce is concerned, is the dominant sector (while agriculture is dominated by the private sector). The public sector subscribes to planned economy.

Oil and Natural Gas

The oil explorations in the disputed border areas between the North and South Yemens have been successful. The prospects of oil exploitation, currently planned to start by 1988, promises the foundation of a more secure economic base for North Yemen.
The exploration activities of the foreign oil companies and the National Petroleum Company of the Yemen Arab Republic have already boosted the economy and it is expected that oil and gas will soon become the major local industry in this country.

It is believed that North Yemen's oil reserves would support a level of production that would permit 100,000 barrels per day (b/d)

*Kawar, S., *IMF Survey,* 5 May 1986, pp. 139-141.

to be exported; unofficial sources put potential exports at 400,000 b/d. In addition, a refinery with a production capacity of about 10,000 b/d – one third of domestic oil needs – has just started operation. The Government is also planning to construct both a 225-mile pipeline extending from the oil fields to the Red Sea and related port facilities; the pipeline could become operational as soon as 1988.

The First Three and Five Year Plans (1974-77 and 1977-82)

The first Three Year Development Plan for 1974-77 and the first Five Year Plan for 1977-82 have contributed to opening up the economy to new developments. Imports rose considerably and most domestic funds were diverted to consumer goods rather than investment. The bulk of expenditure in the first five year plan was spent on infrastructure, including YR1,294 mn ($283 mn) on health and education, which was about 7 per cent of the $3.5 bn total budget. Around 40 per cent of this total sum was provided by loans and grants, with a large percentage from Arab sources. Saudi Arabia, Kuwait, the UAE and Qatar were amongst major contributors.

The Second Five Year Plan (1982-86)

Total budget expenditure for the second Five Year Plan (1982-86) was almost double at $6.4 bn, which was dependent on foreign sources for 50 per cent of its costs. The Second Five Year Plan for 1982-86 aimed to increase investment and to improve the country's existing balance of payments deficit. The main objectives of the 1982-86 Plan were as follows:

(1) Development strategy was guided by the overall goal of establishing a united Yemen state (i.e. the unification of the Yemen Arab Republic with the People's Democratic Republic of Yemen).

(2) This plan stressed the need to increase productivity through the better use of existing resources (especially agriculture).

(3) Greater stress was to be placed on the appropriate development of manpower resources.

(4) A more regionally balanced development approach was sought.

(5) Encouragement of national savings for investments purposes was sought.

(6) There is a push towards self-reliance, with more import-substitution ventures and moves to encourage remittances into investment schemes rather than consumer goods.

18

(7) Encouragement is to be given to the growth of the private sector.

So far as fiscal policies are concerned the two main objectives of the Government are as follows:

(1) to generate sufficient domestic resources which the government can use to continue the modernisation process in the country;

(2) to pursue a fiscal system which is conductive and contributive to the development process by limiting any excess fluctuations in the market forces, and by guiding investments, savings, consumption and production.[6]

Conclusion

In conclusion, North Yemen is the second poorest country in the Middle East region,[7] with a GNP per capita of about U.S.$550. Ever increasing imports (together with goods under-declared or smuggled), reduced remittance earnings and the Dhamar earthquake (with a reconstruction programme costing $630 mn over four years) have all resulted in falling foreign exchange reserves, a restriction on import licences and a scaling back of development goals.

IV POSSIBLE UNIFICATION OF THE TWO YEMENS

In March 1979 a constitutional commission from both the People's Democratic Republic of Yemen and the Yemen Arab Republic was appointed to draw up a constitution for a unified state. A 136 – article draft constitution is expected to be the basis of the unified State of Yemen, but an early unification seems unlikely. The decidedly militant leftist Democratic Yemen would not allow itself to join with the conservative North Yemen as a unified Republic in immediate future. Democratic Yemen accepts unity only within the framework of a "democratic" State i.e. the unity should serve the interests of international socialism.

The campaign for the unification of North and South Yemen began with Imam Yahya. It was later favoured by Egypt which wished to impose its control on the entire Southern Arabian region. More importantly, throughout the civil war the left wingers of both Southern and Northern Yemen freely mixed and co-operated with each other. Thus it has been argued that the political development of both Democratic Yemen and North Yemen, have been part of a single transnational political and ideological movement. The

6. For further discussions, see Chapter 3, sections on commercial law and banking.

7. The poorest country in the Middle East is the People's Democratic Republic of Yemen.

Constitutions of both North and South Yemen emphasise the aim of unification. Indeed, the official names adopted by both countries refer to Yemen as a single unified country. However, various indicators (such as political, economic and social developments in the two Yemens, their foreign policy and international relations) show that the two countries will remain separate political entities for the forseeable future.

The major differences between the two countries can be classified as follows:

First, North Yemen is basically (i.e. over 80 per cent) rural. There are only three major towns (i.e. Sana'a, Ta'izz and Hodeida) in a country with a population of almost nine million. Rural communities are small. By contrast, South Yemen is relatively more urbanised in general, and the Port of Aden is a much more developed centre in particular.

Secondly, North Yemen has a moderate nationalist government closely associated with, and supported by, Saudi Arabia and its allies. South Yemen is a determined Marxist-Leninist regime, firmly committed to its "strategic alliance" with the Soviet Union. Positively anti-Western its radical policies and revolutionary ideas have caused subversion and cross-border warfare in the neighbouring conservative Arab countries.[8]

Thirdly, North Yemen has considerably more people (nine million) than South Yemen (two million), but conversely South Yemen has a larger area.

Among these and other differences, the one which makes a unification of the two Yemens unattainable is their ideologically different form of government and politics. This is not to deny the importance of what the two Yemens have in common in terms of religion, language, Arab identity and tradition. These common features can definitely provide the corner stone of the foundation of a future united Yemen. In the short term, however, what can bring the two Yemens together is their need for foreign financial assistance, primarily from the same sources i.e. the Arab oil producing countries. Since the mid-1970's, more aid from the neighbouring Arab countries has flown into South Yemen, partly as a result of changing security needs in the Gulf.[9] The Gulf Co-

8.   Directly in North Yemen and Oman, and indirectly in other conservative Arab States including Saudi Arabia and its allies in the Gulf Co-operation Council. For details see AMIN, S. H., *Political and Strategic Issues in the Gulf,* Glasgow: Royston, 1984, pp. 39-41, and pp. 34-37.

9.   It is very interesting to note that the independent-minded State of Kuwait has now replaced the revolutionary Libya as South Yemen's main source of foreign finance for social sector development.

operation Council formed in 1981 to provide scope for co-operation amongst the conservative Gulf States, is in itself a positive step towards better relations in the Arabian Peninsula and the political evolution of the countries of this important sub-region. It is thus very encouraging to see that the Gulf Co-operation Council has committed itself to provide more resources for development to both Yemens, in spite of traditional hostilities between the Democratic Yemen and Oman (a founding member of the Gulf Co-operation Council). During the period 1977-81 South Yemen received $352.5 million from a number of Arab funds to cover development in all sectors, while Arab co-financing with inter-national agencies, including the World Bank, provided another $143 million by mid 1983. Co-financing has included aid from AFESD, KFAED, Opec Fund, Abu Dhabi Fund, IFAD and the Islamic Development Bank. This pattern of foreign aid can contri-bute to a more moderate policy in South Yemen and also pave the way for a possible co-operation between the two Yemens. Such co-operations in areas of economic development is quite possible, although full integration and unification may be unattainable because of ideological and politcal differences between the two Yemens.

V. CONCLUSION

The Democratic Yemen is a full member of the Socialist legal system. The Marxist-Leninist regime is organised through the Yemeni Socialist Party designated as the leader and guide of both people and State. In the South, the legal system is being Sovietised and private enterprise is restricted. Social services including free education, free health care and free legal aid and advice are directly afforded to all citizens. By contrast, North Yemen is a conservative Arab State following free market economic policies. The government here is unwilling to intervene and to restrict private enterprise.

Chapter 2

LAW AND JUSTICE IN THE PEOPLE'S DEMOCRATIC REPUBLIC OF YEMEN

I FORM OF GOVERNMENT

1. Form of National Government

The country is officially governed by a "collective leadership" exclusively drawn from a Marxist-Leninist party called the Yemeni Socialist Party. The party has an Executive Committee (the Politburo) which is charged with the administration of the State affairs. The party's Secretary-General is the President of the republic. The institutional structure of the national government is based on 'Scientific Socialism, class struggle and democratic centralism.' Thus theoretically, there is a collective administration. In practice, however, as demonstrated in the civil war of January 1986, it may not be so. The ruling elite often do not wish to share their powers with fellow party officers and seek to free themselves from the administrative and executive constraints imposed by the party structure based on 'democratic centralism'.

The structure of the ruling Yemeni Socialist Party was modified in 1984. The Party Congress in October 1985 favoured further radical policies and indicated somehow a lack of support for the less extreme policies persued by President Ali Naser Muhammad. This resulted in a brutal and destructive civil war in January 1986 between the President's supporters and the advocates of ultra radical policies of "Scientific Socialism". This fighting left more than 15,000 dead and resulted in widespread devastation and destruction. At the same time, the Civil war of January 1986 proved that behind the Democratic Yemen's facade of centralist Marxist-Leninist form of government, lie powerful tribal loyalties, personal animosities and significant differences unreconciled by Marxist-Leninist doctrines and official Party guidelines.

2. Regional and Local Governments

Under the British, the Colony of Aden had three local government bodies: the Aden Municipal Council and the Shaikh Othman and Little Aden Township Authorities. The Aden Municipal Council was an autonomous body with a nominated President and ten nominated and six elected members. Outside the colony of Aden, the British authorities did not administer the

South Yemen

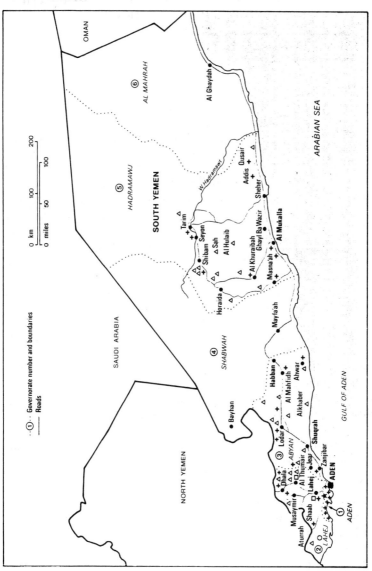

Protectorate territories directly. In each of the two Protectorates there was a British Adviser assisted by a small British and Arab staff. The tribes nominated their own chiefs, subject to confirmation by the Governor of Aden. Not all the chiefs had complete control over their people, but their authority greatly increased by the introduction of simple administrative machinery under the British.

After independence, the country was divided for administrative purposes into seven governorates and twenty eight provinces, each headed by a centrally appointed governor.

3. Elective People's Councils

The participation of citizens in the local and regional levels is sought throught the establishment of a system of elective people's councils aimed at the perfection of mass public organisations. It is in the course of of mass organisation that the socialist regime of the Democratic Yemen has armed the civilian population. Many of these armed civilians have actively served the People's Militia, guard units and People's Defence Committees. The support of the working people for the ruling Communist regime and its policy is more evident in the urban areas. The masses of tribal and village people hardly participate in such political set-ups, but political education may well change the attitude of the younger generation in the forseeable future.

II LEGAL HISTORY

1. Early History

Between 1200 BC and 525 AD, Southern Arabia was part of the Minarean, Sabaean, or Himyarite Kingdoms. It was the Kingdom of Sheba whose queen is said to have visited King Solomon in Jerusalem in the tenth century BC. The area was conquered by Christian Ethiopians in 525 AD and later fell to the Persians. Yemen was conquered by the Muslims in 632 AD and was thus firmly incorporated into the Islamic State. After the third century of the Islamic era, the weakness of the caliphate led to the formation of many "city states" throughout Yemen. In 1538 an Ottoman naval expedition in the Red Sea conquered Aden. Attacking the Upper Yemen the Ottomans struggled to occupy the entire Yemen, reaching San'a in 1547. The North was liberated from the Ottomans by the Zaidi Imams in 1636. Later in 1834 the British occupied the port of Aden in the south and thus the country was divided into three parts: (a) the East and West Aden Protectorates governed under British hegemony, (b) North Yemen governed by

24

the Zaidite Imams, and (c) South Yemen comprising a number of Arab emireates, sheikhdoms, and sultanates including Abdali, Bayhan, Dhala, Audhali, Fadhli, Lower Yaha, and Upper Aulag.

2. British and Colonial Rule

The port of Aden, captured by the British troops from the Abdali Sultan in 1884, became a Residency under the government of Bombay – a situation which lasted till 1932 when control was transferred to the Governor-General of India in Council. Aden was made a Crown Colony in 1937 and its administration was assigned to a Governor and Commander-in-Chief. This constitutional change was made with a view to satisfy the rising political expectation of the native Yemenies without relaxing the direct control of the British government of this strategicly important base. The Governor and Commander-in-Chief were responsible to the Colonial Office, and assisted by an Executive Council composed of the three chief officials and other nominated persons, of whom two were Aden Arabs.[2]

During the period 1944-1963 laws were made by a legislative council in Aden. In 1944 an Order in Council, issued in London, provided for a 'Legislative Council of the Colony of Aden' whose members were selected by the Colonial Office. The Council was inaugurated in 1947, and at the time consisted of the Governor as President, 4 *ex-officio* members, not more than 4 official members, and not more than 8 unofficial members. During 1955 four of the non-official members were made elective, to be voted in by the British subjects only. In 1956 nine members of the Legislative Council were appointed to supervisory posts over various departments such as the Treasury, Education, and Labour. In 1963, the Legislative Council was suspended when the British government declared a state of emergency.

Notwithstanding the British occupation of Aden, the Ottoman Empire continued its claim of sovereignty over Yemen. In 1911 a treaty signed between the Imam of Yemen and the Sultan of Turkey, formally divided the country whereby the jurisdiction of the Imam was confined to the highlands in the North Yemen, leaving the rest of the country – including South Yemen – to the Turkish overlordship. After the collapse of the Ottoman empire in 1918, the Imam of Yemen campaigned for the reunification of Yemen and attempted to extend his rule to South Yemen. This was

---

2. United Kingdom (Naval Intelligence Division), *Western Arabia and the Red Sea*, London, 1946, pp. 276, 309 and 339-341.

stopped by the British who *de facto* controlled the entire southern Arabia. The British remained in control of South Yemen until the early 1960's.

3. Struggle for Independence

The United Kingdom faced a strong popular resistance throughout South Yemen in the early 1960's. As the British had been forced out of Suez, the empire's Middle East Command was transferred to Aden. At the same time the republican regime of North Yemen, supported by Egypt, was positively feeding anti-imperialist sentiments in South Yemen as a result of which a situation of Civil War erupted there. In 1963 the British, declaring a state of emergency, assumed direct colonial rule, bypassing the Legislative Council of the Colony of Aden. Faced with organised opposition, the British Government eventually produced a Defence White Paper in February 1966 which declared the intention of the United Kingdom to withdraw its troops from Aden by the end of 1968. Throughout this period the United Nation's Special Committee on Decolonisation was monitoring the situation as well as sending missions to the area to facilitate the independence of the Southern Arabian territories. As a result, the final withdrawal of the British forces began in August 1967.

Throughout the British rule, both customary law and the Shari'ah were widely applied in the Aden Protectorate along with certain colonial legislation. The British, however, attempted to replace the traditional application of the customary law by a modern and organised hierarchy of Shari'ah courts. Prior to these organisational attempts, the only effective authority within each tribal unit was its chief or Sheikh and within each confederacy the sultan or some local Mansab. The law that the tribal chiefs applied within their jurisdiction was that of ancient custom (and not always the Shari'ah). A system of tribal sanctions prevailed between tribe and tribe, tribe and sultan and confederation and confederation; while any litigation was referred to judges or arbitrators of repute within each community. These traditional judicial authorities made no attempt to enforce their judgments in the modern sense. Their function was limited to hear the case and then declare for which party it was to produce the required witnesses, and which party had to swear oaths upon which they pronounced their verdict. In criminal cases, the Islamic penal code was applied and the ancient law of retribution and/or self help prevailed. Within this system of customary laws, the Islamic legal system made its impact through two separate channels. First, the general principles of Islamic family law had percolated through to the people as a whole and succeeded in amending or even replacing pre-Islamic customs inconsistent therewith; and this would naturally be felt chiefly in the towns. Secondly, the 'judgments' and 'arbitration awards' of local holy men, whether Sayeds from the Hadramaut or *Ulama* from the Yemen, would be primarily based on Islamic law and not customary tribal law.[3]

Before their departure, the British made considerable efforts to promote a constitutional set up as the 'Federation of South Arabia', joining together the six British-controlled States of the Western Aden Protectorate, Bayhan, Fadhli, Aulaqi, Dhala, Lower Yafa and the Upper Aulaqi Sheikhdom. To this end a new treaty, signed in 1959 between the United Kingdom and the Federation, extended British protection to the new State and thus allowed the United Kingdom government to remain fully responsible for the defence and external affairs of the new State. The British protected Federation was formally established in 1962. This arrangement, however, was opposed by the anti-imperialists in both South and North Yemens who received substantive support from the revolutionary Egypt under President Gamal Abdul Naser. The Egyptian President, visiting Sana'a in North Yemen in 1966, pledged to 'expel the British from all parts of the Arabian Peninsula' and campaigned to liberate 'the Occupied Yemeni South'.

During this period of struggle for independence from the United Kingdom, two major political groups, with clear difference in their political and ideological thinking, emerged in South Yemen. The first grouping was composed mostly of intellectual and professional classes and particularly school teachers and trade union activists in the urbanised port of Aden and its surroundings. They fought for a united nationalist regime and, as already said, drew support from the revolutionary Egypt under Naser. This nationalist movement looked up to Naser's United Arab Republic (Egypt, North Yemen and Syria) as their model. The other group, mainly the inhabitants of rural areas and tribal settings in the up-country, advocated a more rigid form of socialist government. They looked towards the orthodox Marxist-Leninism for inspiration and guidance and

---

3.   Anderson, J. N. D., *Islamic Law in Africa,* London: HMSO, 1954, Part 1, Aden and East Africa, p. 11.

considered the Soviet Union as an ideal example. By 1966, the National Front for the Liberation of South Yemen (commonly known as NLF) got the upper hand and defeated the Naserite nationalists.

4. The Post-Independence Era

Having purged the more moderate elements from within its own ranks, the NLF established itself as the sole inheritors of colonial rule. It was thus in the name of a unified liberation movement that the NLF assumed rule of independent South Yemen (1966-67). When the British eventually left the region in 1967, the NLF formally dissolved the 'Federation of South Arabia', declaring the establishment of 'the People's Republic of South Yemen'.

The NLF described itself as a 'popular democratic liberation movement'. This organisation was progressively transformed during the 1966-71 period, both in theory and in practice, into an effective socialist party. Advocating more socialist and leftist policies, the Yemeni ruling party set the country firmly on the road to "scientific socialism". In 1975 the National Front amalgamated with two smaller parties – the Vanguard Party (a Ba'athist regional party independent of the ruling parties in Iraq and Syria) and the communist People's Democratic Union. The aim was to build the "scientific socialism" through the supremacy of this new vanguard party.

The party transformed the southern Yemen into a socialist State, nationalising all viable sectors of the economy and taking full control of the society. In 1978 the ultra radicals asserted themselves and brought to power Abd al-Fattah Ismail, a reputed rigid Marxist. In 1980 President Ismail was forced to resign in favour of a more moderate President (Ali Naser Muhammad) who ruled the country for six years until the civil war of January 1986.

III SOURCES OF LAW

1. Islamic Law

Despite ideological opposition of the Marxist regime to religion and traditional values, in practice, Islamic law and tribal tradition remain the most important source of law in the Democratic Yemen. In point of fact the Constitution of 1970 declares Islam as the State religion, although freedom to practise other religions is guaranteed.* The Shafi'i school of Islamic law is followed by all

---

* This is significant, because certain Arab constitutions e.g. that of Algeria do not provide any express guarantee for freedom of religious practice. See AOUED, A., et Constitutional Law of Algeria, Glasgow: Royston, 1986.

native Arabs in the Democratic Yemen and constitutes a real and profound source of law in this country. Indeed Islam continues to be largely practised and is still formally part of the school curriculum. As a result of these deep-rooted traditional practices and religious teachings, the socialist measures introduced by the government are very slow in taking root in very many areas (including the emancipation of women). The significance of traditional patterns and tribal loyalties was demonstrated in the course of brutal civil war occurring in January 1986. Then the party officials and members of the armed and police forces took side with their tribal people, attaching little importance to socialist doctrines and ideological class struggle.

2. Constitutional Law

The main constitutional instruments are the 1970 Constitution and the 1978 Constitutional Amendment. Immediately after the British withdrawal in 1967 existing ordinances and regulations remained in force. The presidential authority, replacing the powers of the British and Federal governments, was established as the executive organ, while the 141-member National Front general command formed the interim legislative authority. After the expiration in 1969 of the term of office granted to the National Front, a new Constitution was adopted on 30 November 1970 where provisional People's Supreme Assembly (alternatively known as the People's Supreme Council) of 101 selected members took over legislative power.

The Constitution of 1970 proclaimed the country a progressive socialist state and part of a single Yemen and of the Arab nation. This brand of socialism evolved from a nationalist revolution. Thus the Constitution also guaranteed a broad range of civil liberties and human rights including rights to decent housing, free education, medical care, and social security. Furthermore, the Constitution prescribed universal suffrage in the elections of both national and local councils. It described the workers, peasants and petty bourgeosie as the various social classes which were required to participate in the transfer of the country into a socialist State. Hence the constitution refers to 'work' not only as a right of the citizen, but also as his obligation.

The 1970 Constitution also ascribed to planned economy and collectivisation, imposing governmental incursions into socio-economic spheres.

The People's Supreme Assembly was designated as an appointed legislature. It had a membership of 101 persons (extended to 111 in 1978 and to 140 in 1982), 86 selected by local councils and 15 by the trade unions. The first People's Supreme Assembly was appointed in 1971. They were not elected representatives of the population, but were the nominees of local branches of the ruling United Political Organisation National Front (UPONF). In 1972, with the assistance of Soviet advisors, the ruling Party was reorganised in accordance with the principle of 'democratic centralism', emphasising on centralism and vertical control, with a view to create an alliance between workers and peasant masses. In factual terms, however, control of military establishment remained the most decisive element of political power.

In October 1978, the People's Supreme Assembly amended the 1970 Constitution and allowed for the formation of a new party styled the Yemen Socialist Party. This new ruling Party, a successor to the National Front (UPONF), has a secretive and totalitarian character. It is a Marxist-Leninist 'Vanguard' Party based on 'scientific socialism' i.e. a communist model. It has a Political Bureau, an Executive Committee, an Appeals Committee, an Information Committe and a Central Committee (composed of 47 members and 11 candidate members). The Secretary-General of the ruling Party acts as the President of the Republic.

In this way the structure of the executive authority closely follows the Soviet model. The central role of the ruling party is acknowledged in Principle 2 of the 1978 Constitution stating that the party is the 'leader and guide of the society and the State' and it 'should lead the struggle of the people and their mass organisation towards the absolute victory of the Yemeni revolution's strategy . . . '

The new party structure has been designed to create a politburo and presidium form of party-government structure but thus far this has not occurred. The People's Supreme Assembly appoints a 5-man Presidential Council (or Presidum of the Assembly). The chairman of the Presidential Council is the secretary-general of the Yemeni Socialist Party and concurrently serves as the Head of State. Thus the chairman of the Presidential Council stands at the head of the functional side of the government. The State affairs and operational responsibilities are carried out by the various ministries under the leadership of a Prime Minister whose appointment is subject to pro forma approval of the Assembly. The party controls the supreme councils encompassing the regional governorates and their political subdivisions. Officials in the latter realm have been

30

appointed and are generally subservient to the central authority. The party secretary-general (i.e. the Head of State) wields more ideological authority through his control of the Central Committee, Political Bureau, and the subordinate women's, youth's, and labourers' organisations and, most importantly, the independent People's Militia.

3. Legislation

The People's Supreme Assembly exercises legislative power. The membership of the Assembly was extended in 1982 to 140 (from 111 members), elected for a five year term by universal suffrage. The Assembly appoints, from amongst its members, the President, the Prime Minister and the senior judges. Constitutionally the Presidential Council submits draft laws (bills) to the Assembly for debate and ratification. In practice, however, with the Yemen Socialist Party being the only political party, the Assembly is an arm of the executive; it does not, and can not, disagree with the policies formulated by the executive. In point of fact, most of the Assembly's decisions are 'unanimous' (e.g. the re-election of President Ali Abdallah Salih to another 4-year term on 22 May 1983) which emphasises the lack of freedom to vote differently.

4. Usage and Customs

Tribal customs and traditional practices still continue to be of relevance in the legal environment of the Democratic Yemen. There are an estimated 1,400 separate tribes of native Arabs in the country who are still following their own way of life with the least interest in the legal norms and codes adopted by the State.

IV DEVELOPMENT OF THE NATIONAL LEGAL SYSTEM

1. Colonial Legislation

British rule in Aden formally introduced the English common law and equity into the Colony of Aden, imposing colonial rules and standards in the country. However, the areas of law affected by colonial legislation were primarily related to aspects of public law and administrative law and did not change the nature of the private law of the land which was a mixture of customary tribal law and the Islamic legal system.

The colonial legal system was visible in the urbanised Port of Aden where the political, administrative and naval presence of the

A South Yemeni labourer, 1956

Aden Protectorate Levy Fort on North Yemen border; irregular troops in foreground

Arab children at Dhala in 1955

33

British soldier with camel bearers at Lahej, with some of the Sultan's buildings at the background.

British Empire was concentrated. By contrast, the rest of the country remained more or less completely free from any colonial penetration, thus the English common law and equity had made no impact on the social and legal relations of the native Yemenis residing outside the Port of Aden. Nevertheless, some legacies of British legislation are still visible in the legal system.

Illustrative of the more important pieces of legislation promulgated by the British in the Colony of Aden were the following laws: Aden Colony Loan of 1953, Aden Protectorate Levies of 1939, Aden Protectorate Rulers' State Troop of 1940, Authentication of Documents of 1942, Birth, Death and Marriages Registration of 1941, British Nationality of 1950, Census of 1945 and Civil Courts of 1937. As such, the British legislation did not change the nature and character of the legal system in the Southern Arabia. These colonial rules and ordinances were not comprehensive and affected only certain formal and administrative matters, while they left the socio-economic life of the society intact. In this way the legal system of Aden continued to be regulated by customary and tribal law on the one hand, and religious law of

Islam on the other. Nevertheless, the colonial legislature provided a more smooth formal framework for the operation of the existing traditional legal system as well as providing many new norms in areas of substantive law – sometimes with a view to change and rectify the existing legal norm e.g. Law of Divorce (1938) and Child Marriage Restraint (1939). Other important laws on Banking (1952), Bills of Exchange (1941), Carriage of Goods by Sea (1941), Charitable and Religious Trusts (1939), and Contracts (1938) were intended to modernise, reform and standardise the Colony's legal system. Probably the most important of these codes of law was the Law of Contracts Ordinance enacted on 20 December 1938 which consisted of 182 articles dealing with offer and acceptance, voidable, conditional, and void contracts, performance and breach, and quasi-contracts. In this way the law in Aden was reformed, drawing primarily on the British experience of legal reform in the British India.

These well-thought-out British-Yemeni legislation provided the foundation of a modern secular system of law and public administration in the Southern Yemen. However, in spite of the fact that Yemen was one of the last outposts of the British Empire to be relinquished, the British impact on the legal system of this country is by far less than what has been the case of other former British colonies such as India and Pakistan.

2. Post-Independence Legislation

Following the departure of the British from the southern Arabia, Presidential authority replaced the powers of the British and Federal governments. The ruling party of the new independent Yemen retained the basic codes of law, though they made no particular attempt to enforce the colonial legal codes left by the British. In 1976 the revolutionary government promulgated a new secular Penal Code and later a new Criminal Procedure Code, introducing substantive and procedural innovations to the country's legal environment. Furthermore, the Constitution of 1978 pledged the gradual enactment of other codes governing areas of civil, industrial and family law on a nation-wide basis. This constitutional commitment reflected the Government's aspiration to set the country firmly on a socialist path.

2.1 Criminal Law

In addition to its control of the economy, the State has also attempted to influence the legal culture through a new penal code introduced in 1976. In terms of this code legality means conformity to centralism and criminality means conducts unsuitable for building up a Socialist State. It must be mentioned that in spite of this penal code and a large number of other codes which have been officially promulgated by the State, the varied tribes in the country remain outside the reach of State legislation.

Amnesty International, the London-based human rights organisation, published a brief report in 1976 which dealt with political prisoners, detention centres and prisons, alleged torture, and instances of capital punishment and disappearances in the Democratic Yemen. This study shows that the state of criminal justice in the country is far from satisfactory.

2.2 Family Law

In the area of family law, the British had taken several steps to remove customary laws which discriminated against women or exploited children (e.g. Child Marriage Restraint Ordinance of 1939). The post-independence government introduced further legislation in these areas with a view to emancipate Yemeni women. One such piece of legislation was Law no. 1 of 1974 concerning the family.[4] Modelled on the Divorce Law of Tunisia, this Yemeni legislation restricted polygamy by requiring the official permission of the court for second marriage. It also prohibited child marriages and provided for a considerable degree of female protection including equal rights in divorce.

The Tunisian Code's provisions with regard to divorce and marriage are radical; thus fitting to be a model for the South Yemen. Islam permits a husband to repudiate his wife unilaterally and without reference to a court. South Yemen and Tunisia, unlike other Arab countries, have taken the bold step of abolishing the institution of *talaq* completely. Articles 29 and 30 of the Tunisian Code state the rule clearly that: "Divorce is the dissolution of marriage"; " ... a divorce may take place only before a court." Thus, any form of extra-judicial divorce is now invalid. Moreover, the Code gives women equal rights with men in seeking a divorce in the courts.

The modern Tunisian and South Yemen laws of divorce are pretty liberal. They provide three bases upon which a court of law may dissolve a marriage:

4. Ghanem, I., "A note on Law no. 1 of 1974 concerning the Family, People's Democratic Republic of Yemen", 3 *Arabian Studies* (1976), pp. 191-96.

(1) The first basis, roughly comparable to the common-law notion of matrimonial offence," permits a divorce, upon the request of either the husband or
wife, " . . . for reasons specified in the articles of the present Code." The only
particular grounds specified by the Code as definitely giving rise to a divorce are
the failure of the husband to support his wife (Art. 39) and the failure of either
party to perform a condition specified in the marriage contract (Art. 11). While
the Code imposes upon the husband various other obligations such as requiring him to treat his wife with kindness, to live on good terms with her, and
to avoid injuring her, it nowhere specifically states that the failure to live up to
these obligations will constitute sufficient legal grounds for divorce.

(2) As a second basis, the law permits divorce by mutual consent of the spouses.

(3) And, finally, the court may grant a divorce at the request of either husband
or wife, " . . . in which case the court shall determine the damages owing to
the wife as compensation for the injury she has sustained, or what compensation she shall pay to her husband." Thus, either spouse, if persistent enough,
may obtain a divorce upon demand and without proving a specific "matrimonial offence"; however the spouse who obtains a divorce "without cause"
becomes liable to pay a damage remedy.

Principle 27 of the Constitution of 1978 prescribes that the law
should regulate family relations on the basis of equality between
man and women in rights and duties. However, in practice the
process of emancipation of women in Yemen has been very slow
owing to lasting traditions prevailing in this part of the Arabia.
Indeed the tribes of the Democratic Yemen resist not only the
liberalisation of social and family laws but also the leftist policies of
the regime aimed at collectivisation and socio-economic change.

2.3 Laws related to Economy

With a view to prepare the legal environment for socialist
governance, principle 12 of the 1978 Constitution provided that the
State was to own, manage and develop all sectors of the economy in
conformity with the 'substantive laws of scientific socialism'. It
called for applying the fundamental and general rule 'from each
according to his ability and for each according to his work.'
Accordingly in the same year when the Constitution was
promulgated, some 36 foreign interests were nationalised. This
move reaffirmed earlier attempts by the State to take full control of
the country's economy. Soon after the independence, the
government had nationalised most major industrial and trading
organisations; namely:

(a) confiscated, without compensation, the lands belonging to
   big landlords and those of religious endowments,
(b) nationalised residential properties in towns and
(c) took control of fishing industry throughout the country.

2.3.1 Agriculture

The Agrarian Reform and the reorganisation of the land tenure system has meant the abolition of feudal system and the creation of new farming concerns. These included a State-owned agricultural sector and the introduction of farmers/workers co-operatives. The state sector is run with effective assistance provided by the Soviet advisors and technicians.

2.3.2 Fisheries

Any fisheries development programme in the Arabian Peninsula must be directed towards the rational development of the artisanal traditional, small-scale fisheries because 93 per cent of the total catch of the Peninsula is landed from such fisheries. South Yemen by establishing fisherman's cooperatives has begun a process which will give the fishermen better training and education as well as better means of production. For training purposes the Aden-based Institute for Fisheries Training (established in 1970) offers a four-year course in various fields of fisheries as well as short courses to local fishermen. The fourteen or so fishermen's cooperatives provide boats, engines and technical support facilities.

Following the nationalisation of fisheries (1969) and the establishment of fishermen's cooperatives for the development of small-scale fisheries, incorporating more extensive training of fishermen, supported by technical assistance programmes for fishermen, socio-economic conditions in fishermen's communities has slightly improved. These steps taken to organise the small-scale fishermen have been highly politicised. It is hoped that the new cooperatives would allow the fishermen to raise their standard of living, receive better education and training, and more importantly, free themselves from the debts of "middlemen".

2.3.3 Foreign Investment

The 1978 constitution did not outlaw external participation in the economic process. However, it was in 1981 that, as part of President Ali Naser's liberalisation plans, a law on foreign investments was passed. This provided some benefits for investors who, in particular, could draw profits from an enterprise over several years. The law was designed to attract foreign investment particularly from the Yemenis working abroad. It attempted to stimulate private enterprise and to shed some of the leftiest excesses of the early 1970's.

The Ministry of Commerce and Economy holds effective

jurisdiction in respect of the issuing of licences for external capital and workforce participation. A criterion which ensures the approval for foreign investment is evidence to prove that external assistance will fulfil some basic requirement for the economy which cannot be provided locally.

2.3.4 Import Regulations

During Ali Naser Muhammad's tenure of presidency (1980-1986), trade restrictions were eased to allow the importation of building materials and certain itemised goods by private operators. However, most of national trade has remained monopolised by the Government. Indeed very many goods are directly imported by the State-owned corporations. By way of example, the National Drug Company has exclusive rights to import drugs, while the State-owned "14th October" Corporation has a monopoly on all books and publications. The principal state instrumentality in international trade is the National Company for Foreign Trade. This company has an exclusive authority over the importation of a wide variety of goods ranging from dairy products to agricultural machinery, as well as many other items such as textiles, pumps, shoes, fishing gear, and cement.

The Democratic Yemen disallows the importation of certain goods. The list of such prohibited items are specified in the Organisation of Foreign Trade Law No 21 of 1971 and Ministerial Resolution No 12 of 1973. They include matches; kitchen goods; mirrors; nails, paints; wooden or metal furniture; pickles; salt; some tobaccos, and plastic footwear. Trading with Israel and South Africa is also strictly prohibited. Other goods may only be imported if purchased with currency held by a foreign bank.

The import of almost all products requires an import license, though building materials for government projects may now be obtained without a license.

All imported goods must be insured with the State-controlled National Insurances and Re-insurance Corporation without which the bank will not open Letter of Credit or grant foreign exchange control permission. Normal documentation is also required, including a fully detailed invoice and a Certificate of Origin.

There are no limits on the amounts of foreign currency that can be brought into the country or to how much is taken out, so long as it does not exceed that declared on entry. The export of local currency is limited to YD 5 for visitors, with an extra YD 125 in travellers cheques for residents.

According to current regulations, duty is charged on an ad valorem basis on the C and F price of goods. This varies from 10 to 40 per cent for textiles and clothing; 10 per cent for agricultural and industrial machinery; 20 to 25 per cent for spare parts and as much as 30½ per cent for motor cars and vehicles.

2.4 Law of the Sea

One of the areas which has been regulated by modern and secular legislation is various aspects of the law of the sea. The Democratic Yemen, facing the Arabian Sea to the east and the Gulf of Aden to the south, is geographically very advantaged, compared with many other Arab countries, because of its extensive access to open seas. Democratic Yemen's jurisdictional zones off its 1400 km long sea coast, afford this country a very considerable potential for economic exploitation of the living and non-living resources of the sea and the continental shelf. The access to these maritime zones is also of great strategic significance particularly because of this country's control of the Strait of Bab al-Mandab which separates the Red Sea from the Indian Ocean. Mindful of its vital interests in the marine and submarine areas off its coasts the government by enacting the law No. 45 of 1977 extended its territorial sea to 12 nautical miles while declaring an exclusive zone of 200 nautical miles from its coasts as the country's exclusive fishing zone. The law also fixed the outer limit of the country's continental shelf at the outer limit of its continental margin or to a distance of 200 nautical miles – whichever is the greater.[5] With such maritime areas, the Democratic Yemen has a very real opportunity to develop a profitable fishing industry in its exclusive fishing zone and exploit the resources of the seabed within its considerable continental shelf area.

The claim to exclusive rights for the sea resources by South Yemen is aimed at controlling fishing as a "coastal" State; and not based on its being a "maritime" State with actual or potential capacity to exploit the marine resources. However, in addition to these economic reasons there are some political factors involved too. The Strait of Bab al-Mandab, a source of apprehension to Israel, is controlled by South Yemen and the Republic of Djibouti

5. El-Hakim, A. A., *The Middle Eastern States and the Law of the Sea, Manchester:* Manchester University Press, 1979.

(the narrower part of this strait lies entirely within the territorial seas of South Yemen and Djibouti).

The Fisheries Nationalisation Law of 1969 provided a legal framework for collectivisation of the fishing craft and implements as well as the State-sponsored organisation of 14 cooperatives under the Ministry of Fisheries. It is known that the Arabian Sea fishing grounds are among the richest in the world, but until recently South Yemen lacked the material capability to fish its distant marine zones. It is only since 1975 that the government has received financial and expertise assistance from friendly countries such as the USSR, Cuba and Iraq to develop a national fishing industry. Aid has been also given by Denmark, Kuwait and Abu Dhabi for further management of fishing resources. Fish catches and marine products obtained in 1978 amounted to 150,000 tons.

The Public Corporation for Fish Wealth was established in 1970, under the Ministry of Agriculture and Agrarian Reform, as the Government agency responsible for the management and all operations of the industrial fisheries sector, and for the marketing and distribution of fresh fish and fish products for both local and export markets. In November 1977, this Corporation became the Ministry of Fish Wealth. The structure, staffing and responsibilities are the same as in the former Corporation. Basically, the Ministry is involved in management, administration and finance as well as in the operation and maintenance of fishing vessels, canning factories, cold stores and marketing of fish and fish products.

The commercial and industrial fisheries enterprises are based on the use of large vessels, both trawlers and purse seiners. All vessels are owned by the Ministry of Fish Wealth and the catches are landed, processed and marketed also by them, mostly for export.

The only reported exception is a Japanese joint venture to exploit cuttlefish for Japan. There are sixteen vessels for food fish, and one factory-ship. There are also eight purse seiners to exploit the sardine resources as raw material to a floating fish meal barge, a new shore-based plant with 500 tons/day plus an original 150 tons/day shore plant; four other vessels are also run by the Ministry. Total recent landings from these fleets are not available, but exported processed products in 1977 were 6,330 tons. Also under construction, with USSR help, are a canning/freezing cold storage unit (300 tons storage and 15 million cans/year) and a freezer, cold storage ice plant complex (800 tons cold storage, 20 tons/day freezer, 25 tons/day flake ice plant).*

During the late 1970's, fishing was done by the State-sector fishing fleet, fishing co-operatives, the private sector and also foreign (Japanese) and joint (Yemeni-Soviet and Yemeni-Iraqi) companies. Foreign and joint companies, whose catches of fish and sea products were just above 8 per cent of the total volume, accounted for 65 per cent of their value. This is due to the fact that these companies caught the most valuable types of fish and sea products (langoustes and squid), using the most modern vessels and fishing tackle. The state and the private sectors contributed about 80 per cent of all catches, but in terms of value this constituted slightly over 20 per cent, for they netted chiefly fish species of low value. There are plans to expand the fishing and these efforts are directed towards developing a more effective national fishing. It is creating a modern fishing fleet and building fishing ports, refrigerator capacities and processing enterprises, and training national personnel. In this field the Democratic Yemen is actively co-operating with the Soviet Union. The Government aims to raise the processed fish output to 200 tonnes by 1988.

South Yemen, together with North Yemen, Sudan and Somalia, participated in the 1977 Taiz meeting which declared the Red Sea to be a "zone of peace". In a press communique delivered on 7 July 1978 by Mr Muhammad Saleh Mutei, Minister for Foreign Affairs, and circulated as a United Nations communication, the People's Democratic Republic of Yemen delcared that "the Red Sea should remain a zone of permanent peace and security and should not be subject to any foreign influence or domination." Moreover, with regard to the Strait of Bab al-Mandab, "the Government of the People's Democratic Republic of Yemen confirms its respect for the freedom of maritime and air traffic of ships and aircraft of all coastal and non-coastal states, without prejudice to the sovereignty, integrity, security and independence of the Republic."

V JUDICIARY AND DISPUTE RESOLUTION

1. Pre-Independence Judicial System

Traditionally, within clans and tribal communities, local disputes were arbitrated by tribal chiefs who heard cases according to the prevailing customary laws. During the British rule, the

---

* FEIDI, Izzat H., Institutional Aspects of Fisheries Development in the Gulf States and Arabian Peninsula, Rome: Food and Agricultural Organisation of the United Nations, 1978.

Colony of Aden's judiciary became a dual system consisting of colonial civil and criminal courts dealing with commercial, criminal and British Admirality affairs on the one hand, and Shari'ah and/or religious courts on the other.

The colonial courts included a supreme court and a number of subordinate magistrate courts, which were organised along the following lines:

Firstly, the Civil Courts consisted of:

    (a) the Supreme Court presided over by the Chief Justice, with unlimited jurisdiction;

    (b) the Court Registrar (of the Supreme Court) with jurisdiction to hear claims up to the value of 1,000 rials; and

    (c) the Court of Small Causes, i.e. cases not over 500 rials in value, also presided over by the Registrar.

Secondly, Criminal Courts consisted of:

    (a) the Supreme Court, in which all trials, in the British tradition, were by jury; and

    (b) the Chief Magistrate's Court and Divisional Magistrates' Courts, with powers to pronounce a sentence of up to two years' imprisonment or a fine of 1,000 rials.

Thirdly, civil and criminal courts of appeal

    (a) the Supreme Court for hearing appeals against the judgment of inferior courts in the colony,

    (b) the High Court of Judicature at Bombay (and after the independence of India, the British Court of Appeal for Eastern Africa) for appeal from the Supreme Court,

    (c) from the Bombay or East African Court to the Judicial Committee of the Privy Council in London.[7]

The Civil Courts in the Colony exercised their jurisdiction in conformity with usage, and in the absence of usage in conformity with the substance of the common law, the doctrines of equity, the British and Indian statute laws in force when Aden became a colony and the ordinances passed since. In matters of personal status, Muslims, Hindus, Jews, and Parsis applied their own religious and customary laws respectively. In matters of criminal law, the Indian Penal Code was enforced.

2. Post-Independence Judicial System

After independence, the Constitution of 1970 pledged the

---

7. United Kingdom, Naval Intelligence Division, *Western Arabia and the Red Sea*, London, 1946.

reorganisation and unification of the judicial system and the provision of a national court structure. Accordingly the administration of justice was entrusted to the Supreme Court and Provincial Courts. The former, consisting of the Chief Justice and the Puisne Judge, is situated in Aden. The Provincial Courts are situated in the various governates. Within each governate, there are some Divisional Magistrates' Courts.

2.1 Magistrates' Courts

These courts have both civil and criminal jurisdiction. In civil cases they hear all claims not exceeding 1,000 Yemeni dinars, as well as all aspects of workmen's compensation, land and water disputes, and housing claims irrespective of the amount involved. They also have exclusive jurisdiction to hear cases of divorce, maintenance, custody of and access to children and divorce settlements. In criminal cases, the Magistrate Courts can try all cases which are not subject to the exclusive jurisdiction of higher courts. Thus this court hears all minor offences under the Penal Code as well as all traffic offences under the Traffic Law of 1974. Magistrates' Courts also have exclusive jurisdiction to hear crimes committed by juvenile offenders.

2.2 Provincial Courts

As courts of first instance Provincial Courts hear all civil and commercial cases whose value exceed 1,000 Yemeni dinars. Also acting as court of first instance in criminal matters, the Provincial Courts hear all the serious crimes such as murder, manslaughter, rape, arson and gross indecency. As courts of appeal, they hear all appeals from the magistrates' courts within their respective governate including civil and criminal cases.[8]

In addition to this regular judicial structure, two more politicised and powerful courts have been established. First, the People's Supreme State Tribunal, consisting of three members (one appointed by each of the following organisations: (a) the Yemen Socialist Party, (b) the army and (c) the security forces). This Tribunal adjudicates offences against the 'People and the Revolution led by the party', as well as cases affecting the survival and security of the Republic. Secondly, the People's High Court

8. This information is based on what Mr Naguib Shamiry, the President of the Supreme Court in Aden, provided in his presentation to a symposium on contemporary Yemen held in Exeter in July 1983. An edited version of the paper was later published thus SHAMIRY, N., 'The Judicial system in Democratic Yemen', in PRIDHAM, B. R., *Contemporary Yemen,* London: Croom Helm, 1984, pp. 175-194.

(the Security Division of the Supreme Court) consists of a President and two members appointed by the Presidential Council. This Court deals with cases jeopardising the Revolution, the People, and security – trying political prisoners and enemies of State.[9]

3. Arbitration

By the Arbitration Ordinance, promulgated in the Colony of Aden on 19 March 1941, voluntary arbitration was recognised as an alternative to litigation for dispute settlement. Significantly Articles 3 and 17 of this enactment, taken together, make a submission irrevocable and thus allowing the court to stay proceedings where there is a valid submission. If one party declines to appoint the arbitrator, the other party has the right to petition the court for appointing the required arbitrator or arbitrators. The arbitrators have the power to administer oath, hear the evidence and publish an award. However, the award is subject to judicial appeal and if the arbitrator "has misconducted himself", or "an award has been improperly procured", the Court may set aside the award (Article 12). An award once filed in the Court, is enforceable as if it were a decree of the Court (Article 13).

VI THE LEGAL PROFESSION

The legal profession was organised under the British by the Ordinance on Council of Legal Practitioners enacted on 4 November 1954. Article 2 of this Ordinance defined a legal "practitioner" as a pleader in possession of a valid certificate issued under the Supreme Court (Pleaders) Rules and who normally practised before the Supreme Court. This Council, representing the legal profession, was composed of four practitioners elected by the Annual General Meeting of all practitioners. The Council's main tasks and powers were:

(a) to make rules to maintain a high standard of conduct and etiquette among the legal practitioners in the Colony.
(b) to provide information on standards of etiquette and practice, and
(c) to administer and process the admission of new members to the legal profession.

---

9. For a report on the post-independence Yemeni courts, see Joe Stork, 'Socialist revolution in Arabia: a report from the People's Democratic Republic of Yemen', *Middle East Research and Information Project Papers,* paper no. 15, Feb 1973, pp. 1-25.

Immediately after the independence the legal profession was diminished. Later Article 127 of the 1970 Constitution required that the legal profession be regulated by law with a view to provide free legal aid and legal assistance to the citizens and corporations. By the Criminal Procedure Code of 1977 as amended in 1983-84 a system of legal aid was introduced to all criminally accused. By Civil Procedure Code and the Court Fees Law of 1981 legal aid was extended to civil cases as well.

The Law No. 12 of 1982, the Legal Profession Law, regulated the profession. According to these provisions of this new legislation, intending advocates must obtain practising certificates or licences from the Ministry of Justice. These certificates which have to be renewed annually entitle the licensed advocates to practise anywhere in the Republic and appear before all the courts. The law also provides for the organisation of the members of the legal profession through the Council of Advocates. The disciplinary control of the profession is upheld by a quasi-independent committee which includes a representative of the Council of Advocates. This committee is responsible to the Ministry of Justice which takes the final dicision concerning any complaint against an advocate. Under the present regime, there are three categories of legal practitioners in the Democratic Yemer. . First, advocates who are qualified lawyers licensed by the Ministry of Justice. Secondly, Private agents or attorneys in fact who can represent their principals in civil cases. They need no legal qualifications, but they are generally conversant with legal issues and court procedures. Thirdly petition writers who can draft documents and write court petitions in cases where the claim does not exceed 50 Yemeni dinars. However, it should be noted that all documents and petitions exceeding this limit have to be drawn up by Advocates.

VII LEGAL EDUCATION

Legal training and education is very limited indeed in the Democratic Yemen. This should not be surprising in a country which ranks 110th among the nations of the world in its literacy rate. According to the latest statistics, there are no more than 925 primary schools, 37 secondary schools, and 22 institutes of further education to cater for the 2 million population. The only institute of advanced higher education, the University of Aden, was founded in 1975 with five faculties. The University, still in the process of organisation and expansion, plans for law schools which will offer a four year Law Degree and will also train judges, magistrates, clerks and legal practitioners. Currently there is a 'two month' apprenticeship period for training judges. There is also a law institute set up by the USSR in 1974 to train clerks and magistrates for the rural areas. The duration of training was in 1977 increased to three years and it is planned to bring this to four years. The law institutes is to be incorporated into the University of Aden and styled the College of Law.

Conclusion

South Yemen has a Marxist orientation. Its legal system is a mixture of socialist measures and customary traditions. Following its struggle for independence from Great Britain, the victorious NLF adopted a radical programme for the new republic's political and economic evolution. The emphasis was on central control by means of 'scientific socialism'. As an anti-imperialist movement directed against British colonialism, the revolutionaries in Aden refused all the British-sponsored constitutional formats[10].

Marxist-Leninist ideology has made its marks on areas of public law, introducing ideological, political and administrative patterns alien to Yemen. Islamic traditions and tribal customary practices, however, remain dominant in areas of private law. Tribal allegiances and family ties are still more effective than national loyalty. For the majority of the people, the views of the tribal and religious leaders carry a greater weight than the rules and regulations promulgated by the State.

10. One of these proposals was the *Constitutional Proposals for South Arabia 1966*, presented by Sir Ralph Hone and Sir Gawain Bell, Published by the Federation of South Arabia.

Chapter 3

LAW AND JUSTICE IN THE YEMEN ARAB REPUBLIC

I FORM OF GOVERNMENT

1. Early Constitutional Arrangements
Under the Constitutional arrangements of 1962, executive power
was vested in the President of the Republic, Head of State. He was
elected by the Council by a two-thirds majority for a term of five
years. The Vice-President was appointed by the President. The
President promulgated the laws, commanded the Armed Forces,
declared war, concluded peace, had the right of pardon and the
power of appointment. The executive and administrative organ of
the State was the Government consisting of a Council of Ministers
appointed by the President. Ministers had access to the
Consultative Council which could withdraw its confidence from a
Minister. These arrangements were modified by the promulgation
of the Permanent Constitution in 1970 and later by constitutional
developments occurring in 1974.

2. Existing Form of National Government
The Permanent Constitution of 1970 established a Republican
Council whose chairman was to be the President (Articles 73 and
74). The Government was designated (by Article 95) as the
"supreme executive and administrative body of the State", being
composed of the Prime Minister and a number of Ministers.
However, since the suspension of the 1970 Constitution, in terms of
Principle 14 of the Provisional Constitution 1974, the Chairman of
the Command Council, as head of State, has assumed the function
of general sovereignty, particularly in taking the measures he deems
necessary to protect the revolution and the republican regime. At
present the Cabinet is the Executive body of the State, while an
advisory board of senior Government Officials advises the
President. Since 1976 power has been gradually shifted from the
Presidency to the Prime Minister and Cabinet.

Colonel Ibrahim al-Hamdi, who had come to power after a
bloodless coup in June 1974, was assassinated (October 1977). So
did his successor Ahmad Hussein Ghashmi (June 1978). Then a
99-member Consultative Council was appointed by the
Command Council itself, after Colonel Ali Abdullah Saleh came to
power in 1978. The membership of the Council was later

increased to 159 members. Its task is to assist the Command Council which exercises both legislative and executive authorities in terms of Article 15 of the Provisional Constitution of 1974.

The Republican Resolution No. 499 of 1979 established the Bureau of Ifta and Tashri', as a body affiliated to the Presidency and the Council of Ministers. The Bureau is the general department of *Ifta'* (giving *fatwa* i.e. legal opinion pronounced by a Mufti). Composed of a number of high ranking Shari'a scholars, the Bureau also participates in the drafting of legislation. In terms of Article 2 of the Resolution, the Bureau is to state its opinion when so required by the Presidency, the Council of Ministers, the Ministeries and the Public Services. The Bureau helps in drafting treaties, ordinances and advises on constitutional problems, as well as, in appropriate circumstances, on the legal aspects of formation of new public corporations in the country.

3. Regional and Local Government

Administratively, the country is divided into ten provinces (each, in turn divided into several townships and districts). One of the functions of the Governors of the provinces and townships is the enforcement of the judgments issued by the judiciary. Appointed by the Republican Council, the Governors are the principal executives representing the central government within their respective provinces.

II LEGAL HISTORY

For the first two centuries of the Islamic era, Yemen was directly ruled by the Islamic caliphate. Afterwards it was ruled by local dynasties. In 1517 when the Sultan Salim I of Ottomans defeated the Mamluks, the Mamluk commander at San'a accepted the Ottoman Sultan's overlordship. In 1534 the Zaidi Imams established an independent Imamate.[1] The Ottomans twice occupied Yemen but finally Yemen became independent from Ottoman rule in 1918 by a proclamation issued by the late Imam Yahya (reigned 1904-1948). The Imam who ruled both as spiritual and temporal ruler, was assassinated in 1948, and eventually Ahmad Hamid al-Din became Imam. After the death of Imam Ahmad in 1962, and shortly after the succession of his son al-Badar to the office of Imamate, a *coup d'etat* led by Colonel Abdullah al-Sallal established a republican regime. The situation developed into

1. Theoretically, under the Zaidite School, any male citizen of good character is eligible to become imam; but in practice the imamate was thoroughly autocratic and the preserve of a few aristocratic Zaidi families.

49

North Yemen

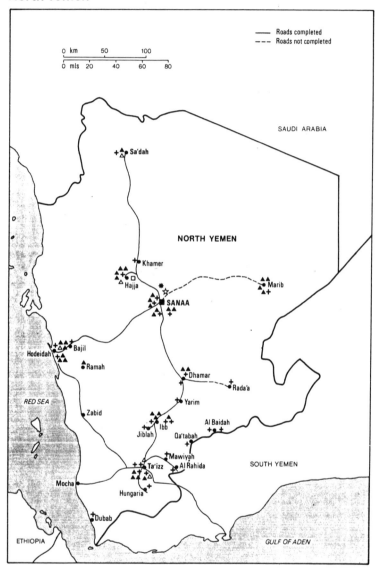

a civil war between the supporters of the ousted Imam and the new rulers (the Imam being supported by Saudi Arabia, Iran and Jordan; while the revolutionaries were supported by military assistance and troops sent to Yemen by the United Arab Republic). Eventually, in 1962 a Provisional Constitution was promulgated, consisting of 155 articles, which declared the secular constitutional arrangements for the Yemen Arab Republic.[2] However, because of the fighting between royalists and republicans the 1962 Constitution did not come into force, and a new constitution had to be promulgated after the reconciliation between the fighting factions in December, 1970.[3] The 1970 Constitution was suspended in 1974 by the military who took the power and issued a Provisional Constitution.[4]

Following the creation of the Yemen Arab Republic and the fall of the previous regime, the revolutionaries, assisted by Egypt, formulated a new government structure influenced by, and patterned after, the regime prevailing in Egypt. State authority was exercised through a Revolutionary Command Council presided over by the President of the Republic. The President and his military officers holding key ministerial ranks were assisted and advised, if not controlled, by Egyptian officers and advisors. The Provisional Constitution of 1962 established a presidential council as the supreme authority with a subordinate Executive Council composed of cabinet ministers.

Until 1969, legislation was promulgated in the form of decrees by the Executive Council acting as "substitute legislature". In 1969 a National Council (consisting of forty five members) was formed to function as legislative organisation. Its membership was drawn primarily from the tribes. It exercised only token legislative power as in point of fact real authority remained with the executive. The 3-man republican council which had ruled the country since 1967 was expanded in 1970 to five seats in order to accommodate the royalist elements who reached a compromise with the republicans. Also the membership of the National Council acting as legislature

2.   The text of the 1962 Constitution has been produced in English by AL-MARYATI, Abid A., *Middle Eastern Constitutions and Electoral Laws,* New York and London: Praegar, 1968, pp. 462-483. The author, however, has recorded the date of the Constitution as at April 1964 instead of 1962. But see PEASLEE, *infra,* note 5.

3.   It is most interesting to note that in spite of these constitutional changes, the government structure has been altered mostly in form and not in substance. The legal system continues to represent a combination of Islamic traditions and modest legal reform.

4.   For the entire text of this document see the section on Sources of Law (Constitutional Law), infra pp. 54-55.

C

was extended from 45 to 63 members.

Further constitutional changes occurred with the introduction of a new constitution in December 1970. The republican council was allowed to fluctuate between three and five members, with the chairman still functioning as a chief of state. However, the national council was abolished in favour of a consultative council of 159 members. Significantly, one-fifth of the council seats could be filled by presidential appointment, while the remaining four-fifths remained elective. Both the national and consultative councils exercised only marginal political influence, representing a proportionately small electorate unused to participatory government.

III SOURCES OF LAW

There are four sources of law in North Yemen:

(a) Islamic Shari'a law;
(b) Constitutional law;
(c) Positive legislation and
(d) *Urf* (custom and usage).

1. *Islamic Law*

By Principle 4 of the Provisional Constitution 1974, the Islamic Shari'a is "the source of all laws". This provision is exactly the same as Article 3 of the Permanent Constitution of 1970 which was in turn exactly identical to Principle 4 of the Constitution of 1962.[5]

This general and universal reliance on the Shari'a represents one of the strongest commitments to Islamic law in the constitutions of the contemporary States in the Muslim world, and the strongest in the Arab world.

Furthermore, Article 152 of the 1970 Constitution envisages the codification of the Shari'a and provides for the establishment of a specialist body to define the provisions of the Shari'a relative to business law. Perhaps more important is Article 153, which states that in cases heard by the judiciary, if there is no State law on the subject, the courts must pass their judgment in accordance with "the general principles of the Shari'a."

The majority of the population in North Yemen are Zaidites. They are a branch of Shi'i Islam who believe that the first Shi'i Imam Ali (considered by the Sunnis as the Fourth Caliph) should

5. For an English translation of the full text of the Constitution of 1962 see PEASLEE, Amos J., *Constitutions of Nations,* The Hague: Martinus Nijhoff, 1966 (third revised edition), Vol. II, pp. 1266-1279.

have been the immediate successor to the Prophet Muhammad. After Ali (*d.* 661 A.D.) and his two sons Hassan and Hussein, the bulk of Shi'as acknwowledged Ali ibn al-Hussein as the fourth Imam. After him a dispute arose as to the identity of the fifth Shi'a Imam. The majority acknowledged Muhammad al-Baqir but the Zaidis declared that the head of the state should be chosen among the descendants of Zaid ibn Ali (*d.* 740 A.D.) who was the son of Ali Zain al-Abidin whom all the Shi'ites regard as the fourth Imam, being the son of Imam Hussein, the second son of Ali. In *fiqh,* the Zaidites hold the system of the Zaid ibn Ali to be valid. It was the Zaidites who founded the state of Yemen. The Zaidites form some 60 per cent of the population in North Yemen, the remaining 40 per cent being Shafi'ites and Isma'ilites.[6]

The Zaidites main differences with the bulk of the Shi'as (the twelvers) derives from one basic point. According to the Zaidite school the office of Imamate is selective in the sense that any candidate belonging to the family of the Prophet can be made an Imam provided that he is an able soldier, brave, learned, pious, generous and free from physical blemish. The twelvers believe that the appointment to Imamate is determined by the will of God according to an express statement (nass) pronounced by the Prophet and other Imams. This major theoretical difference results in two practical differences between the Zaidites and the bulk of the Shi'as. First, the Zaidites do not adhere to the doctrine of 'taqiyya' (concealment of belief), but maintain that one must proclaim his right and fight for it. Secondly, the Zaidites do not believe in a "hidden Imam" which is the Twelfth Imam for the rest of the Shi'as.

The school of law followed by the Zaidites in North Yemen was founded by the eminent Zaidite jurist Imam Hadi (died 298 A.H./918 A.D.). However, in practice there is probably not much difference between the law as administered by Shi'i Zaidis and by Sunni Shafi'is (the latter being the main minority in North Yemen). This is because the Hadawi jurisprudence is the most proximate Shi'ite school to the Sunni schools. At the same time, the Shafi'i school of law is the most proximate Sunni jurisprudence to the Shi'ite schools.

6. The Isma'ilites are Shi'ites, partisans of Isma'il whom they consider to have been the seventh Imam rather than his younger brother, Musa, who is accepted by the Twelvers (the Imamites). Their father, the Sixth Shi'ite Imam, Ja'far-as-Sadiq (*d.* 740 AD), is the last Imam whom both sects recognise. The Isma'ities follow his school of law, but in theology they follow the Batinite doctrines.

7. His full name was Yahya ibn Hassan ibn Qasim ibn Isma'il ibn Hassan ibn Imam Ali ibn Abu Talib (Imam Ali being the first Shi'ite Imam and the fourth Sunni Caliph).

In North Yemen, similar to the situation in Saudi Arabia, Afghanistan, and post-revolution Iran, Islamic law is considered, in practice and in law, as the basic law of the country. Although statutory laws are being enacted in selected areas, the Shari'ah remains enforceable in civil and criminal cases. The statutory enactments were initially confined to administrative, economic and commercial activities – but lately, codified law has been introduced to a larger extent to provide for law of evidence and procedure, the court system, arbitration and similar matters.

2. Constitutional Law

2.1 The 1962 Constitution

Following the 1962 revolution which established a republican regime, the First Provisional Constitution was promulgated on 31 October 1962.[8] This significant document, consisting of 155 Articles, declared Yemen as "an Islamic State, Arab, independent and sovereign" (Article 1). It defined the functions of the legislative, executive and judicial powers as well as the role of the armed forces in the country. The 1962 Constitution also guaranteed a number of political, civil, economic and cultural rights for the Yemeni citizens (Articles 7 to 44).

2.2 The 1970 Constitution

The First Provisional Constitution of 1962 was eventually repealed by the Permanent Constitution of December 1970.[9] The Permanent Constitution, consisting of a preamble and 170 articles, is a very important text, because it attempts to represent a balanced and moderate view of the citizens of North Yemen. Drafted by moderate republican leaders, it was designed to attract the moderate royalists while guarding against Imamate or absolutism. All in all, the Permanent Constitution of 1970 was not different from the Provisional Constitution of 1962 in its main parts. Articles 1 to 5 describe the status and characteristics of the State, while articles 6 to 18 declare the "bases of the society". The Constitution 1970, similar to its 1962 predecessor, guaranteed certain rights, including equality, freedom of association and of the press and the due process of law, for the citizens.

2.3 The 1974 Constitution

The 1970 Constitution was suspended in 1974 and a brief

---

8. See PEASLEE, op cit, for the English translation of the entire document, pp. 1266-1279.
9. For the full text of the 1970 Constitution, see the document section of 25 *Middle East Journal* (1971), pp. 389-401.

Provisional Constitution was declared as follows:

"In the name of the people, the Chairman of the Command Council, having taken cognizance of Command Council Proclamation No. 1 for 1974, Command Council Proclamation No. 4 for 1974 suspending the Constitution, and Command Council Proclamation No. 5 for 1974 increasing the membership of the Command Council, and desiring to consolidate the bases of authority during the transitional period and to regulate the rights and duties of all persons in a manner conductive to fruitful production to raise the country to a level which we all hope it will attain, we announce in the name of the people that during the transitional period the country will be governed in accordance with the following rules:

"Article 1. Yemen is an Arab, Islamic and independent state enjoying full sovereignty. Its system is republican. The Yemen people are a part of the Arab nation.

Article 2. The people are the source of all authority.

Article 3. Islam is the state religion and Arabic the official state language.

Article 4. The Islamic Shari'ah is the source of all laws.

Article 5. Yemen is an indivisible territory and its defence is the sacred duty of all citizens.

Article 6. Yemenis have equal rights and public duties.

Article 7. Personal freedom is guaranteed in accordance with the provisions of the law.

Article 8. There shall be no crime and no penalty except as laid down by law and there shall be no penalty for acts except those committed after the promulgation of the law.

Article 9. Homes are inviolable; it is therefore inadmissable to enter them except in such instances as prescribed by the law.

Article 10. The confiscation of private property is prohibited, except within the confines of the law.

Article 11. No person's property shall be expropriated except in the public interest, in the instances prescribed by the law, and with just compensation to the interested person.

Article 12. The citizens have the right to express their thoughts by means of speech, writing or voting within the confines of the law.

Article 13. Places of worship and learning have immunity which cannot be violated except in instances required by security needs and as prescribed by the law.

Article 14. Chairman of the Command Council as Head of State, assumes the function of general sovereign.

Article 15. The Command Council shall assume the functions of the legislative and executive authorities of the State. It shall have the power to lay down general policy and define its general framework."

3. Legislation

3.1. The Legislature

Article 46 of the Constitution of 1962 designated the Consultative Council (Majlis al-Shura), as the supreme legislative body of the State. Elected for three years (Article 49), its members were to consider, pass or reject the Government-introduced bills, as well as initiating the legislation themselves. The President, however, was given the power to dissolve the Consultative Council (Article 87).

The status of the Consultative Council as the organ to exercise the legislative power was retained in the new Constitution of 1970 (Article 44). The 1970 constitutional document also stipulated that the Consultative Council was to be composed of 159 members, freely and democratically elected – but (similar to the 1962 constitution) the Chairman of the Republican Council retained under the provisions of Article 71, the power to dissolve the Consultative Council. In 1974, the Command Council dissolved the constitutional arrangements and in 1978 a People's Constituent Assembly was formed to replace the Command Council. For the time being, therefore, the Consultative Council remains dissolved.

3.2 The Legislative Enactments

There has been a spurt of legislation since the founding of the Republic. The *tashrihat* (collection of enactments) contain the main laws and regulations promulgated by the State. These are directly published by the Government in the Official Gazette of the Yemen Arab Republic. One of the major statutes enacted by the Consultative Council is the Civil Code of 1973-1979. Other important statutory laws, promulgated since this include the Commercial Code of 1976, the Law of Evidence 1976, Family Law 1978, Law of Judicial Authority 1979, Criminal Procedure Code 1979, Law of the Shari'a Grievance Board 1981, the Civil Procedure Code 1981, and the Law of Arbitration 1981. Generally, models from other Arab countries are followed, notably legislation from Egypt, Kuwait and Syria.

4. Customary and Tribal Practices

The tribal society of North Yemen continues to be ruled in very many areas of social life by the traditional rules and customs of the Yemeni tribes. These rules and traditions differ from one tribe to another and from one locality to another. Thus, in addition to the other formal sources of law, customary law is still applied, in spite of attempts by the government to stop such practices which still prevail in the countryside. By ancient pre-Islamic tribal law (i.e. *urf* or *adah*), an *'aqil* may, within a tribe, settle cases of debt, personal quarrels, and disputes about land and water rights, and he may be paid for so doing. Tribal law was intended to keep the balance by application of sanctions to those who have, either intentionally or accidentally, caused damage to others, whereas Islamic law is basically an ideal code of behaviour with a wider scope and purpose than a simple customary legal system. In this way, the customary law may be in conflict with the principles of Islamic law, and thus it will be considered as "irregular." By contrast, when the customary law is not contrary to the principles of the Shari'a, it will be honoured.

Customary law is unwritten and is passed through oral traditions. As an independent legal system, competing with Islamic law, the Imams of Yemen attempted to stop its application. They referred to it as *taghut* (a term used to describe forces against Allah). Imam Qasim (d. 1619 A.D.) ruled that any tribe who follows customary law in substitution of the Shari'a was to be considered as infidels at war with Muslims (*dar al-harb*). In spite of all their determined efforts, the Imams failed to stop the enforcement of the customary law. In other words, the Yemeni tribes refused to abandon customary law in favour of the Shari'a. After the fall of the Imamate, the authority of the central government became weaker. This meant that the northern and eastern tribes could, in the republican era, apply their respective customary law even more than they had done under the pre-revolutionary regime.

IV DEVELOPMENT OF THE NATIONAL LEGAL SYSTEM

Chapter 7 of the permanent Constitution of 1970 provides several constitutional principles concerning the country's judicial system. While Article 144 guarantees the independence of the judiciary, Article 145 provides that judges are independent and are subject only to the Law, and no other authority may interfere in the affairs and matters concerning justice. Furthermore, Article 146 provides that no one is to be appointed judge unless he is learned the laws of Islamic Shari'a and of good character and reputation. Again Article 147 provides that the law appoints judicial authorities and specifies the hierarchy and the jurisdictions. More importantly Article 152 provides that the rules of the Islamic Shari'a concerned with transactions must be codified on the basis of the text (verse of the Qur'an or direction of the Prophet) or juristic consensus *(ijma')* and the law appoints a technical committee to undertake that task. It was resloved by the Cabinet in 1971 that a committee of judges, theologians and law graduates should convene for the purpose. Finally, Article 153 provides that the courts decide cases in accordance with the provisions of the Constitution and the laws of the State, and in the event of a lacuna the decision is to be based on the general principles of the Islamic Shari'a.[10]

10. These 1970 constitutional provisions replaced those provided in the Provisional Constitution of 1962

Notwithstanding the above-mentioned constitutional principles which give great weight to the traditional Islamic Shari'a, the Yemen Arab Republic has gradually introduced several new codes of law dealing with various aspects of commercial law, trade, company formation, commercial agencies, taxation, customs, import and export, banking, arbitration and many other areas.

1. Criminal Law and Tort

In line with the traditional Islamic law, the North Yemeni legal system does not readily recognise a firm division of wrongs into crimes on the one hand and civil wrongs or torts on the other hand. This is why we have used the sub-heading 'criminal law and tort.'

North Yemen is still dominated by Islamic criminal justice, although it is working on the setting up of a modern judicial system in other branches of law e.g. banking and finance (see below). Criminal law and tort, however, is the domain of Islamic law. For instance, when a motorist kills a pedestrian, the tribe of the deceased are entitled, according to the Islamic criminal justice, to receive *diya* (blood money). In Islam a victim or his heirs and representatives are entitled to claim *diya* in certain circumstances including (a) premedidated murder, (b) seemingly premedidated murder, (c) erronous murder, (d) intended offences other than homicide, and (e) unintended offences other than homicide. These Islamic penalties are generally upheld and widely practised in North Yemen, particularly because the alternative Islamic penalty of *qisas* (retribution) is considered as solving no problem. The State, however, has restricted the amount of *diya*, as from December 1976, to 60,000 Yemeni rials in the case of intentional or semi-intentional killings and to 48,000 Yemeni rials for purely accidental ones. In theory however, the tribe may still prosecute the driver and seek retribution instead of demanding compensation.

Quite independent from the Islamic penal justice, many customary and tribal practices are still upheld amongst Bedouins, tribesmen and peasants who constitute a majority of the North Yemen's population. Believing in a concept of 'unity of the tribal blood', members of a tribe are jointly liable for the civil and criminal wrongs committed by any of its membership. Following the same notion, the blood of one member of the tribe allows such a tribe to redeem the crime or tort of another. In short, a person guilty of a capital crime is not alone in his criminal liability but all adult members of his family and tribe through the fifth generation are held liable as well. In the meantime the tribe has a traditional duty to protect any of its members who have committed a crime from being caught and punished by the tribe of the victim. Thus a tribe does its best to prevent any revenge or punishment inflicted on its own criminal membership, as a matter of customary honour.[11]

Notwithstanding the foregoing, the North Yemeni regime is determined to establish a codified system of penal justice universally applicable to all parts of the Republic. The government promulgated a Criminal Procedure Code (Law No. 7 of 27 February 1979) as the basic legislation pertaining to criminal justice. This code is to be applied to all Yemeni citizens, irrespective of their religious and tribal affiliation.[12]

Yorguy Hakim, an Arab legal researcher with the Law Library of Congress as Washington D.C., has translated and reviewed the Criminal Procedure Code 1979.[13] We shall rely largely on his report here in trying to discuss the main features of this very important code which reflects the fundamental principles of penal justice in North Yemen. The basic tenet is that a person is innocent until proven guilty. Indeed this has been guaranteed for all citizens in terms of Article 24 of the Constitution. Furthermore, the 1979 code guarantees complete liberty of defence for the accused. However, the law also accords the judge freedom to deal with any case not bound by any precedent or condition in seeking the truth. In the absence of jury system, the criminal judge receives evidence and will be deciding both on facts and law. Another important feature of the Criminal Procedure Code of 1979 is the significance attached to a unilateral (may be uncollaborated even) confession of the accused. This is a reflection of Islamic rule of criminal justice stating that "the confession of sane persons against themselves is competent.[14] However, once the alleged criminal confesses his crime, the investigating judge should inquire about other evidence that may substantiate the case because "confession alone is an evidence that may sustain controversy like any other type of evidence" (article 40 of the Prosecutor General No. 39 of March 26, 1979). Nevertheless, the Court is free to pronounce its sentence solely on the accused's confession treated as unqualified

---

11. For more details see CHELHOD, Joseph, "*La societe Yemenite et le droit*", *L'Homme*, Paris, April-June 1975, p.72.

12. Yemen Arab Republic, *Official Gazette*, no.2 supp. of 28 February 1979.

13. HAKIM, Yorguy, *Yemen Arab Republic: A Country Law Study*, Washington DC, 1985, pp. 19-28.

14. Eqrar al-uqala ala anfosehem ja'iz.

acknowledgment of guilt. In the case of a partial confession by pleading through counsel, the court should continue to investigate the case and hear the testimony of witnesses. In conclusion, therefore, it is ultimately up to the trial judge to assess the admissibility and validity of a confession by the accused. Thus a confession, like any other evidence in a criminal case, depends upon the discretion and evaluation of the judge in accordance with article 315 of the Criminal Procedure Code. If the judge later discovers that the accused's confession is unfounded, he may dismiss the confession and continue the investigation of the case. Confession must be voluntary.

Arrest Procedure

In accordance with articles 96 and 107 of the Code of Criminal Procedure, 1979, an arrest is defined as holding a person and bringing him before the court or before the prosecuting department or judicial police. Generally an arrest warrant is issued. If the arresting person was present before the representative of the judicial authority, a warrantless arrest is proper. Arrested persons are held in a place other than that reserved for those already convicted, and they must be treated as though innocent. No bodily or mental harm is permitted to extract a confession from those arrested. The arrest order must be signed by the ordering official. The order may be made orally if it is implemented in the presence of the ordering person. The official who issues orders of arrest in any other circumstance is held responsible.[15]

The arrested individual must be notified of the reasons for his arrest. He is entitled to see the warrant for his arrest and to contact a lawyer or other person. If the order for arrest is issued within the limits of the law, it is to be carried out throughout the Republic, on its ships, and in aircraft. An official may be requested to make an arrest outside the area of his jurisdiction. If the arrest is made outside his jurisdiction, he must surrender the arrested person to the local prosecuting department in order to take the adequate procedural precautions.

The law provides that the official who executes the arrest is entitled to use necessary force and to overcome any resistance by the arrested person or by another. Excessive force is not permitted. Consideration of such action is left to the court. The arresting officer may enter the residence of the suspect. He may also enter the

15. HAKIM, Y., op cit, pp.19-20.

domicile of another if there is strong presumption that the accused is hiding there. The owner of that residence or any person there must allow the authorities to enter and must provide reasonable assistance to the search. If the property owner refuses to allow the search, the representative of the authority may use reasonable force to gain entry.

Once the order of arrest is issued, the oficer may search the arrested person and confiscate any weapons. If the arrested is a woman, the searching should be done by a woman. The arrest order may contain a provision for freeing the person arrested on bond. If not, the arresting officer accompanies the suspect immediately to the ordering officer.

There are other circumstances which require the criminal court and the prosecuting department to issue an arrest order against an accused or to subpoena him if they find strong evidence against him (art. 108). If the accused did not respond to the subpoena for a valid reason, the investigator may issue a warrant of arrest to bring him before the court regardless of whether the offence imposes a precautionary imprisonment (art. 109).

The Code of Criminal Procedure strictly limits those instances when person, houses, mail, cables, and telephone communication may be searched or tapped. Article 116 emphasises that these have a certain inviolability. The law also provides that during the investigation the accused may call witnesses and compel the defendant to state his case. Cross-examination of the witnesses and confrontation are guaranteed.

Indictments

Criminal justice relies on the judge's freedom to reach a conviction during the trial proceedings in accordance with article 303 of the Criminal Procedure Code. However, the same article states that the judge is not permitted to form his judgment on evidence that has not been introduced in an open court. This is a very important feature of Islamic judicial principles because in Islam there is no jury as in the case of western systems.

Rights of the Accused

Article 2 of the Criminal Procedure Code of 1979 stipulates that . . . the accused is innocent until proven guilty and penalty is not pronounced unless a trial has taken place in accordance with the provisions of the law whereby the freedom of defence is safeguarded. Any procedure that violates the rights of the accused for his defence is considered absolutely void.

The Criminal Procedure Code provides that no person may be arrested or imprisoned without a warrant issued by the proper authority. The person in custody is entitled to read the warrant and to have access to a lawyer. He must be treated in a way which preserves his dignity, and he must not be injured physically or mentally . Any deposition given by him and proved to be exacted from him or from any witness under coercion, torture, or threat is considered void according to article 99.

If women are in the house, tradition requires no entry and disturbance (article 100). Judicial police are competent to take into custody certain persons pursued by the judicial authorities for having committed felonies or violent crimes. They are also entitled to take into custody any person who has no known address or residence, who tries to hide to avoid questioning, who refuses to disclose his identity, who refuses to go to a police station, or who is caught in a state of drunkenness (article 104). Article 110 on the other hand, provides that any citizen's home and private life are to be immune from any interference, surveillance, or search, and that each person is free to move, travel abroad, and participate in meetings and gatherings without restrictions (art. 5-7).[16]

Representation and Professional Privilege

The accused may implement his defence by himself or through an attorney, either hired or provided by the court, depending on the seriousness of the crime. Information exchanged between the accused and his attorney is considered confidential. Article 137 of the Criminal Procedure Code 1979 states:

> "The investigator is not allowed to confiscate from the defender of the accused or the expert counsel any papers of affidavits the accused has released to them for the implementation of their mission, nor the letters exchanged between them in the case."

As indicated by Yorguy Hakim, the Syrian scholar who has undertaken the translation of this article, we can deduce from these provisions that this "professional privilege" covers not only documents which the accused has surrrendered to his lawyers, but correspondence as well.

Another important protection of the confidentiality of the accused's secrets is that they may not be disclosed by his lawyer even though the accused has confessed information concerning the crime. The law exempts the lawyer from any penalty from receiving

16. HAKIM, Y., op cit, at 21-23.

such information (art. 156). On the contrary, anyone who discloses a secret received in professional confidence or in any other circumstance allowed by law, or anyone who uses that secret for his own beneift or for the benefit of a third person without express permission is liable for one year in prison and a 2,000 rial fine.

Trial Procedure/Procedural Safeguards

In court, the defendant may defend himself. He is also entitled to know what has been said during the course of the trial. If he is a foreigner and does not understand the Arabic language, the court must provide the accused with a translator, in accordance with article 278 of the Criminal Procedure Code.

The accused should be given the opportunity to present his defence and to be the last one to speak *de jure* on his own behalf. He may appeal the sentence to an appellate court (art. 247).

Substantive Criminal Law and Penalties

Available sources do not disclose that there is a code on substantive criminal law in North Yemen. We are again indebted to Yorguy Hakim who has produced the most recent report on this topic.[17] According to him offences and felonies are dealt with in accordance with provisions mentioned in the Code of Criminal Procedure, which contains certain guidelines on both substantive and procedural aspects of criminal law.

When a sentence of capital punishment or severance of limb has been pronounced by the court, the Prosecuting Department must bring the case to the attention of the High Court of Cassation. With that opinion, the execution of such sentences requires the approval of the President of the Republic (art. 339). However, such penalties will not be implemented if the President of the Republic or any other authority who possesses the right of pardon exercises it (art. 409).

In additional to capital punishment, there are the penalties of hanging, stoning, decapitation, and death by firing squad provided for in articles 407 to 413 of the Code of Criminal Procedure. Penalties for severing the right hand and leg and flogging are provided for in articles 415 and 418 of the same Code.[18]

17. HAKIM, Y., op cit, pp25-28.
18. These penalties are based on Islamic penal law. For more details see AMIN, S.H., *Islamic Law in Contemporary World,* 1985, pp.21-37.

Sexual Offences

Severe penalties are incurred for sexual and moral offences under Islamic law. Prostitution, abortion, homosexual practices, indecent conducts and pornographic publications are illegal in North Yemen.

Islam is suspicious of personal pleasures and prohibits any sexual relationships between unmarried persons. Adultery (*zina*) requires death for both the male and the female.[19] Also if a man has intercourse with an animal (bestiality) he is liable to death and the animal to burning. Homosexuals are liable to the death penalty but strict evidence is required for being found guilty. False accusation of unlawful intercourse (*qadhf*) is punishable by death.

Substance Abuse

Consumption of alcohol is strictly forbidden in the Qu'ran. Public drunkenness is punishable by six months in jail. The convicted person may stay in jail as long as it takes the President of the Republic to ratify the sentence, which may also include public flogging, in accordance with Circular No. 1 of January 17, 1980.[20]

Except perhaps amongst the poorest people, addiction to *qat* is universal. The tree known as *catha edulis* of the *celastraceae* family is widely cultivated.[21] Almost all men, women, and children chew the young leaves, leaf buds and tender shoots of *qat*. Every house has at least one *qat* –chewing room and much time is spent in it. During several centuries of its tradtional use, *qat* has had a very negative effect on the economy of the country and on the health of its people. Also in economic terms, *qat* cultivation has been practised to the detriment of the coffee tree. The latter is uprooted and *qat* is planted instead as it is more profitable. North Yemen has no sanctions against its use, although South Yemen has prohibited *qad* – chewing during the weekdays (Saturday to Thursdays).

Violent Crimes

Although available sources do not permit speculation on the statistics for violent crimes committed in the Yemen Arab

---

19. Abu al-Hasan Abd Allah Ibn al-Murtada, 4 *Sharh al-Azhā* (Interpreatation of the Flowers) 336 (Cairo) (in Arabic) as referred to by HAKIM, op cit, p.26.

20. No. 1 of The Official Gazette, January 1980, p.52-53.

21. AYYUB, Muhammad al-Sayyid, *al-Yaman bayn al-Qàt wa-Fasàd qabl Al-Thawrah* (Yemen Between *Qat* and the Governmebt Corruption Before the Revolution (Cairo, 1963) (in Arabic). The best report on the culture of qat appears in U.K. *Western Arabia and the Red Sea*, 1946, *pp.492-93*.

Republic, we may safely suggest that only very limited number of criminals are tried by the State judiciary. Many crimes are still dealt with according to customary law or the Islamic law – outside the formal judicial system.

Despite rigidity of penalties prescribed in the Qur'an for theft or robbery, the penalty of mutilation for theft has been acknowledged in theory but ignored in practice.[22] This was due to the Zaydi attitude of flexibility in dealing with modern circumstances: "provisions change according to changing circumstances." Nevertheless, Zaydites and Sahfi'ites, and other Muslim sects claiming the Qur'an as their ultimate source differ in their treatment of homicide, blood money (diya) and other aspects of customary laws.

Most villagers are inclined to carry arms, such as the rifle and the dagger, for use in tribal warfare, self-defence, vendettas, and as ornaments. The government banned carrying all kinds of arms inside the cities of the Republic with Presidential Decree No. 8 of January 25, 1979.[23]

2. Family Law

The North Yemeni family law is dominated by tribal customs and local tradtions as influenced and modified by Islamic law. Women have a distinctly lower status in the society and the laws regulating marriage, divorce, inheritance and family relationships perpetuate the *staus quo*. Child marriage and bigamy are the norm. 85 per cent of women work on the land.[24]

North Yemen has introduced certain legislation with a view to reform the existing customary practices in the field of family law and domestic relationships. The law sometimes simply aims to standardise the practices or to regulate the irregular practices. We try to discuss various aspects of family law in the light of these new legislative acts.

Marriage

The Family Law of 1978 is the main legislation in this field.[25] The law generally codifies the traditional Islamic law without any substantive deviation or radical reform. This may well be the best

---

22. HAKIM, op cit, p.27

23. Tashri'at, 1980, *at* 63, as reported by HAKIM, op cit, at p.27.

24. According to official estimates, 65 per cent of all women are married (through the good offices of their parents and relatives arranging a suitable match) by the age of thirteen years.

25. North Yemen, *Tashri'at,* 1978, at 91.

course of action because the existing domestic relations are in many ways and in many parts of the country still based on the pre-Islamic tradtions. However, a system of registration is introduced and also the age of majority has been increased.

> *Article 3* Marriage is concluded in a single council sitting whereby a male adult pronounces the offer of marriage according to customs and the counterpart accepts it. Offer and acceptance should not be tied to a term. Any other condition that is not related to the aim of the couple is void.

> *Article 5* The contract of marriage may be concluded by pronunciation or in writing by a letter from a non-present person provided that this letter is read in the Council that received it.
> The contract is valid if it is initiated by a deaf-mute by a signal that indicates marriage.

> *Article 6* The presence of two competent Muslim adult witnesses is necessary to make a valid contract of marriage.

The 1978 legislation also confirms polygamy as acknowledged by Islam. Article 9 states expressively that a man may take four wives if he has the ability to do justice to all.

Registration Requirements

Article 11 of the Family Law 1978 provides that the person empowered to draw the marriage contract (often a religious functionary), the husband, the representative of the wife, and her guardian should register the marriage contract with the competent authority within one week from the date of contract. Otherwise, each one of them is liable for a penalty provided in the Criminal Code. In this way a civil registration system has been introduced into North Yemen, although most marriages still remain unregistered.

Age of Majority

Article 50 of the Civil Code 1979 increased the age of majority to fifteen years.[26] Provided the person is mentally competent, anyone who reaches the age of fifteen is capable of entering into any type of contact including marriage. If upon reaching the age of majority one is in a state of insanity, he will be treated as a non-distinguising child. If a child has not reach the distinguising age or reach it while he is in a state of insanity or retardation, he has no capacity at all.

The Family Law 1978 introduces some reform by providing that marrying a male child who has not reached the age of fifteen is invalid even if his guardian accepts a contract (art. 19). However, if the guardian of a female child concludes a marriage contract on her

26. North Yemen, *Tashri'at,* 1980, at p.122.

behalf, that contract is valid on the condition of her consent after reaching the age of majority. It is not permitted to be alone with her or to marry her (without registration) or to penetrate her unless she reached the age of sixteen and she is able to sustain intercourse.

Anyone who contravenes these provisions is liable to a jail term of not less than one year and not more than three years in addition to what may be retribution for the crime.

Prohibition and Impediments

Articles 21 to 26 of the Family Law of 1978, numerate the causes for prohibition of marriage according to Islamic law. These are classified into two areas: 1) relationship and 2) suckling. Article 21 reads as follows:

> The relations with whom a husband is prohibited (to have sexual relationships) (include) his paternal ascendants and descendants, their wives and those descendants from his parents and the descendants of his grandfathers and the parents of his wife and their branches.

Prohibitions on marriage are applied also to a woman who is breast-feeding an infant (during its first two year's of life).

> A man is forbidden to marry a woman who:
>
> 1. is of a religion other than his unless she belongs to a scriptural religion (Christianity or Judaism);
>
> 2. is an apostate from the religion of Islam;
>
> 3. is married ot another person;
>
> 4. has been accused of adultery;
>
> 5. is a trice-divorced wife before marrying another husbnd and getting her divorce from him and observing her waiting period;
>
> 6. is in her waiting period in an irrevocable divorce from another husband;
>
> 7. is observing a pilgrimage;
>
> 8. is a person whose womanhood is not determined;
>
> 9. is the wife of a missing person before she is released from her matrimonial ties with her missing husband.

He is also prohibited to marry more than four wives. A Muslim woman cannot marry a non-Muslim.

Male Dowry and Extra

The institution of *mahr* (dowry given to the wife by the husband) is still very dominant. The prospective husband, or his family, is required to undertake certain financial obligations in favour of the prospective bride and her family. The requirement of *mahr* is essential under Islamic law, but it is generally considered as a protection for the wife in case of divorce. That is to say that the

67

actual delivery/payment of *mahr* is not demanded by the wife unless she is being divorced. This practice is almost universally accepted throughout the entire Muslim world. To this 'legal' requirement of *mahr,* many Muslim families, particularly those living in tribal settings, often add several other customary marriage payments. In North Yemen, in addition to *mahr* the bridegroom has three other financial obligations. The first is the *shart* (stipulation) which is a sum in cash paid by the groom to the father or guardian of the bride. The second is called *sadaq* (bride price) which is again a sum in cash payable directly to the bride herself. The third financial burden of the groom relates to giving a wardrobe *(Kiswa)* and worthy gifts (particularly jewellery) to the bride, as well as presents to all members of her family and select close relatives. In addition to all these, the groom and/or his family is liable to pay for the celebration feast and wedding party (all such expenses are collectively called *gharamat*). The bride's father or guardian is not obligated to provide presents and gifts – but he usually does. Not by law, but by custom it is expected that a bride brings a dowry worth no less than the amount paid by the husband in the name of *shart.*

The size of these marriage payements vary considerably, reflecting the wealth, social status and future prospects of the groom and the bride – as well as their families. The Islamic notion of *Kafa'* (suitability, competence and sufficiency of marriage partners) is generally taken to mean equality of social standing between spouses and their respective families. This has made the Yemeni society very birth-conscious – thus greatly restricting social mobility through marriage. In the meantime, because of the high rate of inflation as well as the influx of the remittance by those Yemenis working in the oil rich Arab countries, the marriage payments have considerably increased. The government has tried to fix a ceiling on the sums demanded for marriage, but this has been so far unsuccessful.

The 'preferred' marriage is considered to be a parallel cousin marriage where a man marries the daughter of his father's brother. As such in North Yemen tribes, a young man has more or less an automatic right to his cousin's hand. Such 'preferred marriages' count for around 10 per cent of all marriages in North Yemen. The main advantage of this inter-marriage is the fact that marriage payments are considerably lower between close families, compared with those demanded from total strangers.

Requirements for Support of Children and Spouse

Chapter 3 of the 1978 Family Law governs how a husband and wife would live together in accordance with the conditions set in the marriage contract. The Family Law states the following:[27]

Article 27 The husband is entitled to require from the wife her obedience in any way to achieve the interests of the family, especially that she:

1) cohabits in the matrimonial home, unless there is a clause in the contract to remain in her house or in the house of her parents whereby she must allow him to live with her and enter her quarters;

2) make herself available for legitimate intercourse without the presence of any person.

3) carry out his wishes and fulfill her work in the house of matrimony;

4) never leave the house of matrimony without his permission. However, the husband cannot forbid his wife to go out if she has a legitimate excuse or if custom dictates and if there is nothing to bring dishonour or disregard to her duties toward him especially when she goes out to care for her assets or to perform her duty. Caring for her aged parents is considered a legitimate excuse when there is no one else to serve.

Article 38 The wife shall be considered a run-away if she no longer obeys her husband. She will not be considered so in the following circumstances:

1) if the husband did not pay the advance amount of her dowry;

2) if he did not prepare the legal residence for her;

3) if she does not feel security for herself and for her assets with him;

4) if he refuses to support her and it was not possible to carry out the court decision concerning her alimony because he has no visible means of support.

Article 39 The husband must provide his wife with the following:

1) a legitimate dwelling suitable for both;

2) expenses and clothes for her;

3) justice between her and the other wives covering expenses and housing if they have gathered in one house.

Article 40 It is required that the legitimate dwelling should be independent (and be a place) where the wife find security for herself and for her assets, taking into consideration the social standing of the husband, the dwelling of his peers, city customs, and the protection of the wife. The husband may live in one house with his wife and her children whether they are born to her or to another wife even if they are adult. His parents and the women prohibited to him may also live with him if their housing is his duty, unless this causes the wife any stress if such a condition was not provided for in the contract.

Furthermore, the husband should provide for his revocably divorced wife during her waiting period and for the divorced pregnant wife until she delivers her child. Alimony takes

---

27. Translation taken from HAKIM, Yorguy, *Yemen Arab Republic: A Country Law Study,* Washington DC, 1975, pp. 35-36 with some modification by this author.

Yemeni infantrymen

Women bringing camel-dung for fuel into San'ā

70

Boys of the Yemeni highlands

*Long-headed type of yemen
highland official*

Jewish boy at San'ā

71

precedence over all other obligations the husband sustains according to Family Law of 1978.

The Law also provides alimony for children and for indigent relatives. Alimony may also be charged to a rich son for the support of indigent or sick parents (art. 153).

Status of Illegitimate Children and Adoption

There are no provisions in the Family Law of 1978 concerning the status of illegitimate children except article 114 which states:

> *Article 114* The afilitation of a child is confirmed to his/her mother simply by affirmation of his/her birth (even without her acknowledgment and without any restriction or conditions).

Acknowledment of a child of unknown parenthood can be legitimised if the would-be father or mother has not been contested by the child or if common sense, custom, or the sacred law do not contradict acknowledgment. Article 116 of the Family Law of 1978 makes it illegal for a father to proclaim that his child was born of adultery.

Islam does not recognise adoption and Article 127 of the Family Law confirms that:

> "Parenthood is not legitimised by adoption even if the adoptee was of unknown parents".

The illegitimate child has no family relationship but his own. Neither his natural father, his natural mother, nor their descendants may inherit from him. Conversely he cannot claim any inheritance from them. Only legitimate children may qualify as heirs, and when there are not legitimate children, an estate is forfeited to the government. Therefore, adultery, under Islamic law, eliminates acknowledgment of paternity.

Abandonment

When a child is abandoned by his parents because the natural parents do not want their adultery known, any person who finds the child is required by religion to care for him. The finder is entitled to exercise restricted paternal authority over the foundling. If two people have found an abandoned child, the Shari'a judge decides who is qualified to better serve and care for the child.[28] Article 159 of the Family Law recommends what is best for the founding in accordance with the Shari'ah.

---

28. Abd al-Hamid al-Shirwāni, *Tuhfat al-Muhtāi fi-Sharh al-Minhāi (The Needy's Jewel in Explaining the Method)* 367 (Cairo, 1982) (in Arabic) as produced by Hakim, op cit, p.38.

Divorce

By Article 41 of the Family Law of 1978 marriage may be terminated by annulment, divorce, or death.

Annulment of marriage may be implemented only by a court decision. Both husband and wife may seek cancellation of their marriage if there are legitimate grounds for their request such as the presence of a physical defect in the wife or insanity or leprosy in either person (art. 45). Apostasy of the husband or the wife may prompt annulment of marriage, and conversion of a wife to Islam and refusal of the husband to do likewise allows the judge to cancel their marriage (art. 47). Alcoholism is grounds for annulment.

The annulment of marriage is followed in the Family Law by the chapter on divorce defined in article 57, which states that divorce takes place according to a special formula.

Divorce in Islam is the husband's right but the wife may divorce her husband if the right is conceded to her in the marriage contract. The divorce is a pronouncement of a formula such as "I divorce thee" or "My wife is divorced." This pronouncement may be made twice by one party and called "revocable." This means that the husband may take back his wife by word or sign with or without her approval during the waiting period of 90 days. But, if he pronounces the formula three times, matrimony is ended immediately. He cannot take her back unless she marries another husband, is divorced after consummation of marriage and remarries her first husband by a new contract and a new dower (art. 68 of the Family Law).[29]

3. Laws Related to Economy

By contrast to aspects of criminal and family law discussed above, the commercial law of the Yemen Arab Republic has been brought in line with the rest of the modern world. To demonstrate this point we refer to selected aspects of commercial activities in this country.

3.1 Banking Law and Practice

3.1.1 General Background

The North Yemeni banking system is patterned after the conventional Western system. This meas that the country formally sanctions interest-bearing banking operation – notwithstanding the

29. HAKIM, op cit, pp.38-39.

traditional prohibition of interest and usury under Islamic law. Indeed, in spite of the advent of the Islamic banking and finance throughout the Muslim world, North Yemen has not been participating to date in Islamic banking.[30]

The first modern bank in the Yemen Arab Republic was the Yemen Bank. The Yemen Bank (with a 51 per cent State shareholding), was created by a government decree after the new republican regime nationalised the Saudi National Commercial Bank. The new government also set up the Yemen Currency Board which was responsible for the issue of the national currency and acted *inter alia* as a central bank until the establishment of the Central Bank in 1971.

During the 1970's when business and trade were expanding, the Bank encouraged the establishment of joint banks, such as the Yemen-Kuwait Bank and the Yemen International Bank. The equities of these two banks were shared by the Yemen Bank, local businessmen and foreign participants, such as Kuwaitis, Saudis and the Bank of America. The purpose of these two new banks was to promote international banking and foreign investment.

Central Bank of North Yemen

(Millions Yemeni rial)	*1982*	*1981*	*1980*
Foreign Assets	2,436.1	4,350.1	5,779.5
Domestic Assets (Government)	9,647.6	5,520.2	2,727.5
Domestic Assets (Public Entities)	729.7	882.9	627.3
Domestic Assets (Commercial Banks)	42.9	37.9	73.2
Reserve Money	10,279.1	7,439.0	6,894.5
Foreign Liabilities	79.5	71.5	8.9
Government Deposits	1,163.8	1,068.0	694.4
Other Items	1,181.8	917.8	1,025.0

3.1.2. Central Bank

In July 1971, the Central Bank Law transferred the responsibilities of the Currency Board (the issuing of banknotes and the administration of the government's gold reserves and foreign currency accounts) to the Central Bank. The Law also transferred all local accounts, loans and aid to the government –

---

30. The concept of Islamic banking is an original idea developed by religious-minded Muslims with a view to avoid *riba* (interest). For details see AMIN, S. H., *Islamic Banking and Finance,* Glasgow: Royston, 1986.

which had previously been held by the Yemen Bank – to the Central Bank. Thus the Central Bank began to control all banking activities in the country and it was authorised to regulate and supervise the banking operations undertaken by other banks within the jurisdiction of the Yemen Arab Republic. As such it was required from all banks within the country (both domestic and foreign banks operating in North Yemen) to open accounts and deposit their legal and commercial reserves with the Central Bank.

3.1.3. Commercial Banks

The Yemen Bank was originally designed to introduce commercial banking services on the one hand and finance development projects on the other. However, as the Yemen Bank was the only bank in the country, it took over the government's accounts, channelled its foreign loans and aid, and financed its expenditures. Thus this bank practically took on the activities of a Central Bank as well as a development and commercial bank. As a development bank, the Yemen Bank participated in the creation of several quasi-public corporations whose share capitals were provided jointly by both the public and private sectors. The Petroleum Company, the Foreign Trade Company, the Drug Company, the Tobacco and Matches Company and the National Electricity Company were all established during the 1980's by the Yemen Bank which was both the promoter and major shareholder of these companies. These development and financial activities helped to increase commerce and business in the public and private sectors of the economy.

3.1.4. Specialised Banks

As part of development programmes of the Three Year Plan for 1974-77 and Five Year Development Plan for 1977-82, the government introduced specialised banks to serve the different sectors of the economy, such as agriculture, industry and housing. Thus the Government-owned Agricultural Credit Bank was established in 1975 with a capital of 100 million Yemeni rials. This bank began to give direct loans to farmers to develop their farms. Later in 1976, the Industrial Bank of Yemen was established by the government with the purpose of financing and developing industrial projects in the country. Again another specialised bank, namely the Housing Credit Bank, not only gave private loans to individual citizens to build their own homes, but also built blocks of houses which it then sold to individuals.[31]

3.1.5. Exchange Control

Exchange control was first introduced in 1984. The Central Bank of Yemen, and several commercial banks are authorised to deal in foreign exchange. Transactions are handled by the banks with the Central Bank determining daily exchange rates on the basis of London currency market rates. So far as international trade is concerned, all imports require licences, issued by the Ministry of Supply and Trade. This licence ensures the holder may obtain the necessary foreign exchange. Certain categories of imports, however are subject to the monopoly of the State agencies (chiefly petroleum products, medical supplies, and cigarettes).

A comprehensive foreign exchange budget has been operating since 1984. This requires private importers to finance their imports with foreign exchange purchased from local banks and to lodge

1970/81 Indicators of Changes in the Standard of Living in North Yemen

	1970/71	*1975/76*	*1980/81*
		(Yemen rials at 1981 prices)	
Per capita real GDP	1,192	1,537	1,915
		(Yemen rials at 1981 prices)	
Per capita real private consumption	1,194	1,912	2,082
		(million kilowatt hours)	
Installed electricity generation capacity	8	13	64
		(kilometers)	
Paved roads	. . .	916	1,924
		(number of lines)	
Telephone service	. . .	15,915	90,350
		(thousand tons)	
Port handling capacity	. . .	1,700	2,732
		(thousands)	
School enrollment	93	276	453
Population per physician	. . .	17,709	8,649
Population per hospital bed	. . .	2,107	1,725

Data: Yemen Arab Republic, Central Planning Organisation, and World Bank

(Taken from INF Survey, 5 May 1986)

31. For details of various banking operations in the Yemen Arab Republic, see SAQQAF, Abdul-Aziz (ed), *The Means of Mobilising Domestic Financial Resources in the YAR,* Proceedings of San'a' University Symposium, 12-14 Dec. 1982.

import deposits when arranging for import financing. Also the North Yemeni currency has steadily depreciated against all hard currencies. In spite of this a black market for foreign currency has developed with considerable differential between the official exchange rate fixed by the Central Bank and what is available for the transfer of remittances from abroad. All this resulted in a decision by the Central Bank in February 1985 whereby it is required that the financing of all but essential Government imports be carried out at the free market rate.

3.2 Insurance

The concept of insurance was not approved by the majority of the Sunni doctors of law until comparatively recently. However, while all Muslim States gradually recognised the need for insurance services and consequently treated the subject as lawful and valid, the North Yemen was left behind until the early 1970's. This was, of course, mostly due to the economic underdevelopment of the country as well as the historical isolation imposed on the North Yemen by the Imams who ruled there till 1962.

While the contemporary Yemeni law, allows the insurance industry to offer its services in the country, there are still very few persons who seek insurance protection for anything.[32]

3.3 Foreign Investment

The Yemeni Company for Industrial Development, acting in accordance with the provisions laid down and codified by Law No. 13 of 1970, is the principal body responsible for the attraction, guidance, and regulation of foreign investment. The government has been able to attract some new private investments by granting a range of corporate incentives, including a five-year tax holiday, and customs duty exemptions, to project investment exceeding certain levels of investment. Again as concession and incentives, the law allows foreign employees to remit up to 50 per cent of their salaries abroad, and company profits may be freely repatriated. Foreign ownership of freehold land is severly restricted. All operating organisations, having received the necessary government licensing, must submit their books (including a profit and loss account) to the appropriate authority for regular examination. The government itself operates a general pricing code, and foreign investors are obliged to co-operate with such policies.

32. For a general account of the law of insurance in Islam, see AMIN, S. H., *Islamic Law in the Contemporary World*, Glasgow, 1984, pp. 71-84.

3.4 Import Regulations

The Yemen Arab Republic operates a relatively liberal trading policy, restrictions being kept to a minimum. Only commodities from South Africa, Israel and companies on the Arab League boycott list are completely prohibited, together with certain specific items – such as non-medicinal spirits, alcohol, pork products, salt, cotton, obscene literature and privately imported arms.

The import of certain commodities is the monopoly of Government agencies. For example, tobacco products are only purchased by the National Tobacco and Matches Company, arms and ammunition may only be imported by the armed forces via the Council of Ministers, and all imports of petroleum products are similarly confined to the state-controlled Yemen Petroleum Company. By contrast, the import of drugs and medical equipment is unregulated in spite of the existence of the State-owned Yemen Drug Company. Since 1983, however, the government has imposed some restriction on import licences for drugs and pharmaceuticals because the country had become a target for drug dumping. Nevertheless, private enterprise is still free to import drugs and medical equipments.

Similarly, there are no restrictions on the modes of international trade. By way of example, there are no government regulations for barter and countertrade in North Yemen. Thus private interests are free to countertrade at their own discretion.

4. Law of the Sea

North Yemen claims a 6 mile contiguous maritime zone beyond its 12 mile-territorial sea limits (Decree No. 15 of 1967). This contiguous zone relates to security, navigation, fiscal and sanity matters. North Yemen has also asserted its exclusive rights to the continental shelf on the basis of a depth of 200 metres and exploitability test (Decree No. 16 dated 30th April, 1967). Recently, however, this country has extended its exclusively fishing zone to 200 miles.

The Red Sea is vital for North Yemen in terms of maritime security and commerce. North Yemen is also a littoral state of the strait of Bab al-Mandab (with potential control over movement through the strait, especially since it controls several islands in the area, such as Antufash, Urmak, Uqban, Kutama, and Kamaran which she occupied in 1972). The Red Sea is North Yemen's only outlet to the oceans. There are three ports in the area: Hodeida, Mocha, and Salif, of which the most important is Hodeida.

Hodeida has been deepened and expanded, and will probably be further expanded. Mocha can be used only by small ships but there have been plans for its improvement. With the expansion of salt mining at Salif, that port is being rebuilt to enable it to take ships of up to 5,000 tons. Since Hodeida suffers badly from silting, there have been tentative plans to develop Salif into the country's main port.[33]

V JUDICIARY

1. General Background

Traditionally, the Imam of Yemen had been personally performing the various functions of the executive and the judiciary in accordance with the Islamic law principles. In practice, prior to 1962, there was a dual system in North Yemen. First, the Civil Law as administered by the *'amil,* from whom appeal could be made to the Imam; and secondly, the Shari'ah administered by the *hakim,* from whom there was right of appeal, with permission of the local *'amil,* to another *hakim.* Any further appeal must go to the court of appeal in San'a, and from there though rarely, to the Imam.

When the *hakim* tried the case, as in the majority of instances, the complainant obtained a summons from the *'amil.* Should the defendent fail to appear, he was arrested. Witnesses were sworn either before the *hakim* or in mosque; if the complainant had no witnesses he took the hand of the *hakim* and took the oath. The parties shared the payment of fees for the hearing, which depend on the length of the case. *Hakims,* however, were often venal.

After the establishment of the republican regime in 1962, the various constitutional instruments promulgated in North Yemen stressed the independence of the judiciary. By way of example, Article 144 of the Permanent Constitution of 1970 described the judiciary as "an independent authority". Beyond this general statement, however, no especial provisions were made to re-organise the judicial system.[34]

2. Organisation of Courts

There are two categories of courts in North Yemen, the regular courts and the specialised courts.

---

33. Lapidoth – Eschellacher, Ruth, *The Red Sea and the Gulf of Aden,* 1982, pp.61-72.

34. For a good account of the judiciary up to 1972 see zein al-Abdin, T., *The Role of Islam in the State, YAR (1940-1972),* Ph.D. thesis, Cambridge, 1975, Chapter 4, pp.174-205.

2.1. Regular Shari'a Courts

The Shari'a Courts have universal jurisdiction to hear all civil and criminal cases, except those cases which are specifically reserved for specialised courts (e.g. commercial cases, road traffic, tax and customs, immigration and crimes bearing on national security). The Law of Judicial Authority of 21 February 1976, established four courts as parts of a single judicial system: Courts of Summary Jurisdiction, Courts of First Instance, Courts of First Instance and Appeal, and the High Court of Appeal and Cassation. This legislation was repealed by a new Law of Judicial Authority on 20 September 1979. We shall discuss this legislation in more detail.

The current legislation applying to the organisation of courts is contained in the Law of Judicial Authority No. 28 of September 20, 1979.[35] Chapter II of this Law provides for the classification and constitution of the courts. Article 2 reads as follows:

Art. 2 The courts are composed of:
  a) The High Court of Cassation
  b) Courts of Appeal at the provinces
  c) Preliminary Courts.[36]

The above mentioned courts each has a prescribed jurisdiction in accordance with the law. Judicial power is vested in the Supreme Council of Justice composed of (a) the President of the Republic or his deputy, (b) the Minister of Justice, (c) the President of the Cassation Court, (d) two deputies of the Cassation Court, (e) the Legislative Advisor of the state or his deputy, (f) the Prosecutor General, (g) the Vice Minister of Justice, and (h) two qualified members appointed to the post (art. 115).

According to article 122, the Supreme Council of Justice is entrusted to deal with the following matters:

1) propose the general policy for the development of judicial matters;

2) give its opinion regarding the magistrates and their integrity; ·

3) review the annual report forwarded by the Minister of Justice concerning the judges and the courts and the Prosecuting Department and their staff;

4) decide in all matters referred to the Council with regard to the appointment of judges, their promotion, removal, retirement, and transfer from one court to another (the opinion of the Council is final);

---

35. Arab Yemen Republic, *Tashri'at* (official gazette), 1980, p.167.

36. As produced, and translated into English, for the first time in HAKIM, Yorguy, *Yemen Arab Republic: A Country Law Study,* Washington DC: Library of Congress, 1985, pp.12-17.

5) study all the draft laws and regulations issued by the Minister of Justice and the Prosecuting Department before sending them to the Council of Ministers;

6) review the draft of the budget of the judicial authority and give its opinion.

According to the 1979 legislation, the judicial system consists of the following regular courts.

2.1.1 The High Court of Cassation

This Cassation Court sits in the capital. It consists of a president, two deputies, and a sufficient number of judges. The Minister of Justice, after consultation with the President of the Court and approval of the High Council of Justice, forms the following branches: Civil Chamber, Commercial Chamber, Personal Status Chamber, Criminal Chamber, and Examination of Court Decision Chamber. The President, or one of his deputies, or a senior magistrate presides over each chamber.

The Court of Cassation is composed of seventy magistrates from whome the President and deputy are selected. It is assisted by a technical office headed by a president who is selected from the High Court and a sufficient number of judges. The Minister of Justice, after consultation with the High Court President and approval of the High Council of Justice, selects the president and a member of this technical office for a one-year renewable term.

The responsibility of the technical office consists of the following: analysing the judicial principles approved by the High Court of Cassation, publishing a compilation of decisions in booklets and periodical circulars, preparing technical topics, participating in technical preparation of the Court's program, and supervising the library (art. 5).

The General Assembly of the High Court of Cassation is composed of the President of the Court, his two deputies, and the court magistrates. Its duties are set out by law.

2.1.2 The Appellate Courts

Each provincial capital has an appellate court with a president and an appropriate number of judges. The Minister of Justice determines their number after consultation with the President of the Appellate Court and approval of the High Council of Justice. The High Court of Justice may integrate all or part of one province's appellate court's jurisdiction with that of another (art. 7).

The appellate court of one province may convene inside or

outside the venue of its jurisdiction according to the decision of the Minister of Justice after consultation with the President of the Court of Cassation (article 7, paragraph 2).

Provincial appellate court proceedings are conducted by three magistrates. Their decisions are taken by majority vote.

2.1.3 Preliminary Courts

Within the jurisdiction of each provincial appellate court, preliminary courts are established in the capitals of the districts *(alwiyah)* and in the counties *(nawahi)*. These courts have only one judge each.

The Minister of Justice grants local jurisdiction to these courts with corroboration of the President of the Court of Cassation and with approval of the High Council of Justice.

It appears that the new Law of Judicial Authority emphasised in detail the function of the Appellate Court and the Court of Cassation but did not dwell enough on the lower courts whose functions are most important in any judicial system. The reason for this omission seems to lie in the complex social differences among the various factions of the Yemeni population. As legislators observed these difficulties, they tried to remedy the point of contention in articles 8 and 9 of the Law of Judicial Authority No. 28 of 1979. The articles read as follows:

Art. 8 Within the realm of competence of each Appellate Court of a province, preliminary courts shall be established in the capitals of the provinces and districts. Each of these courts shall be presided by one judge.

The establishment of these courts, designation of their quarters, and de-limitation of their local jurisdiction is decided by a decree from the Minister of Justice in consultation with the President of the Court of Cassation and approval of the High Council of Justice.[37]

2.2. Specialised Courts

There have been many administrative tribunals for many years, with exclusive jurisdiction for certain issues such as tax, immigration and customs. More recently in 1976, two new specialised courts of Traffic Courts and Commercial Courts were established to deal with traffic violations and disputes arising from commercial transactions. The Commercial Courts which are still partly staffed by non-Yemenis (often qualified lawyers for other

37. HAKIM, Yorguy, ibid, pp.11-14.

parts of the Arab World particularly Egypt and South Yemen), are in practice perhaps the most important of all specialised courts, so far as private interests are concerned.

In addition to the above-mentioned courts, there is also a Constitutional Court, extablished by Article 155 of the 1970 Constitution, composed of an unidentified number of "Shari'ah scholars of high qualifications."

Another court (perhaps better termed as an administrative tribunal) must be formed in terms of Article 154 of the Constitution 1970 to deal with maladministration.

Article 9 of the Law of Judicial Authority of 1979 states that:

"The establishment of specialised preliminary courts in the capitals of the provinces may be enacted by a decree of the Minister of Justice upon approval by the High Council of Justice. These courts will be competent to deal with a determined category of cases".

A major specialised tribunal is the Shari'a Grievance Board, established under Presidential Decree No. 6 of February 28, 1981.[38] The Shari'a Grievance Board has the authority to hear any citizen's complaints and those of other government agencies in order to assist the judicial system in articulating the problems that confront it, in alleviating its many burdens, in scrutinising a citizen's complaints and the circumstances which forced him to resort to the state, and in evaluating the strength or the weakness of his case (art. 4). If the Board finds that the complainant did not rely on legal authority or that certain procedural technicalities were not observed, the Board must inform the complainant by a reasoned letter of rejecting his complaint, or it must advise him of the proper recourse. Additionally, the Grievance Board expedites treatment of complaints and executes a Shari'a court decision within thirty days following the sentence. If this is not done, the Board allows the complainant to present his case to the President of the Republic, who will decide the case or order trial of the officials who failed to execute the decision.[39]

VI THE LEGAL PROFESSION

In accordance with tradition, most litigants represent themselves in North Yemen personally. There is, however, a rather loosely-organised legal profession which represent the litigants. These self-

38. Yemen Arab Republic, The Official Gazette, No. 2 of February, 28 1981, p.16-19 as produced by HAKIM, op cit, pp.17-18.
39. Ibid.

D

styled attorneys have no formal legal training, but are normally well-versed in the ways of the local courts and are experienced in matters of litigation. It is only fairly recently that these law agents have been required to register with the Ministry of Justice. There is a recent legislation governing the legal profession which provides that future attorneys must undergo formal training.

Judges of the regular Shari'a courts are appointed from amongst the graduates of the *Jamaa (Great Mosque),* the traditional Islamic sources and theological schools. After recruitment, they usually undergo a period of training in the Supreme Court of Appeal. Having completed their training, they will be appointed to lower courts of first instance in various districts. As admission to higher ranks of judiciary is governed by seniority and experience, the judges usually begin their judicial careers in the districts and gradually qualify for promotion to higher courts.

Article 146 of the 1970 Constitution states that no one shall occupy a judicial post except scholars in the Shari'a law, of sound character and behaviour. Furthermore, under Article 149, before assuming his duties, a judge must take an oath by Allah to judge the people justly.

VII LEGAL EDUCATION

Until it was closed in 1964, al-Madrasah al-Ilmiyyah (founded by Imam Yahya in San'a in 1925) was the highest institution of higher education in Yemen. Its students who were instructed, inter alia, in the Hadawi school of Islamic law, were prepared to serve as judges and senior government officials. They were required to study for at least ten years before graduation. Immediately after the revolution, this Madrasah was closed and all other establishments of religious learning were contemptuously neglected.

After the revolution, Kuwait financed the establishment of the University of San'a (November 1970.) The first two faculties which were formed were (a) the Faculty of Shari'a and Law and (b) the Faculty of Letters and Education.

Since the establishment of the University of San'a in 1970 and the subsequent creation of a Faculty of Shari'a and law, aspiring lawyers must read a four year course covering both Islamic law and modern law and legal systems. To be admitted as a practitioner, the graduates must serve under a registered lawyer for a period before

84

being granted right of audience. Admission to higher courts requires longer periods of apprenticeship.

Lawyers must register with a Committee of the Ministry of Justice and the Legal Advisors Office to obtain official permission to practise.

Conclusion

After a period of revolution and civil war, the quasi-theoratic monarchial system of Imamate came to an end in 1962. For some eight years the monarchists resisted the republic. By adopting a constitution in 1970, the moderate republicans compromised with moderate monarchist. This constitutional document was an attempt to reconcile the progressive idealists with religious-minded traditionalists. Officially non-alligned, theYAR is more identifiable with the world capitalist system. It is committed to establish a new order on modernist reformist patterns of development. The republicans fought against the native tyranny of Imamate which had sought to legitimise itself on the basis of Islamic faith. Having divorced themselves from that, the republicans resorted to secularism and nationalism. However, having no clear ideological basis which could attract the native population, the republicans failed to establish their legitimacy. Political power is exercised in automatic fashion led by a militancy elite.

The legal system is still basically Islamic, particularly in areas of private law. However, secularism is now on ascendency. At present codification is in progress with a view to bring this country's system in line with other modernist developing countires. These legal reforms are intended to develop nation-wide norms and standards at the expense of tribal and traditional practices.

Chapter 4

CONCLUSION

In discussing the substantive areas of law and justice, the two Yemens seem to have much in common. These two basically tribal societies, have a common language (Arabic) and a common religion (Islam). They also share quite a lot of the deep-rooted traditions and practices common to the inhabitants of Southern Arabia. These commonalities have been long realised by the Yemenies in both sides and cited in support of the old-age campaign for a unified Yemen.*

A closer examination of the two Yemeni societies and in particular the nature, pattern and aim of their respective constitutional institutions, national and local administrations, foreign relations and public policies, clearly indicates that the two Yemens are completely different in their constitutional and legal structure. Historically, South Yemen and particularly the Port of Aden was much influenced by the British legal and administrative innovation. By contrast, North Yemen was, under the Imams, an insular underdeveloped country, closed to outside influence. More recently, after their respective revolutions, the two parts of Yemen have chosen totally different roads for their future development. Capitalism in the North and Socialism in the South. Thus it must be accepted that the affinity in law and justice has become more confined to areas of private law (principally based on Islamic law) as the difference in areas of public law has increased.

The two Yemeni societies outwardly show considerable institutional change in their respective chosen road to future development. However, to emphasise on these formal and outwardly features can be dangerously misleading.

The contemporary legal system of the Democratic Yemen is a mixture of socialist elements, Islamic law, tribal customary laws and certain aspects of the colonial order. Over the years since attaining independence from the British colonial rule, the State's authority has been progressively extended in all aspects of life. The State intervention in the economic, commercial and social spheres is particularly evident in the urbanised parts of the country. The rural and tribal communities still remain relatively free from State

* See the section on Possible Unification of the two Yemen, discussed in Chapter 1.

penetration into their socio-economic patterns – although farmers and fishermen's cooperatives are familiar features even in rural areas. Government intervention has often resulted in better and wider benefits to the community at national level, but inevitably upsetting the existing socio-economic patterns. For instance, South Yemen does not encourage private practice by medical and legal professionals. This is aimed at providing free medical care and legal aid to all citizens which would ultimately be to the good of community at large. This restraint on the professional private practice, however, has meant that many trained professionals have gradually left South Yemen for the North where private practice booms.

South Yemen basically follows an independent socialist policy. It has developed a socialist system based on Marxism-Leninism and proletarian internationalism. This country's socialism grew out of a mainly nationalist revolution. While the Arab nationalist factor was dominant during the 1960's in the course of struggling for independence, the current thinking in the Democratic Yemen is dominated by socialist internationalism. In attempting to build up a socialist legal order, the Democratic Yemen has been looking to the USSR as a model. The Soviet Union has assisted South Yemen in training its judges for rural areas, professional personnel and public administrators throughout the country as well as party officials. As such the Democratic Yemen is the only Muslim country which has developed and institutionalised Marxist ideas and practices. Fostered by the Soviet Union and other socialist countries, the Democratic Yemen has been a full member of the socialist camp during the past twenty years (1967-87). It seems that the transformation of the Democratic Yemen into a socialist country is already irreversible.

The political reorganisation of society was marked by the foundation of the Yemen Socialist Party in 1978. This well-organised party, set up with the assistance of Soviet advisors, is firmly in control of State affairs. It is supported by professional party workers capable of running a government deeply committed to scientific socialism. As such the Democratic Yemen was the very first Muslim populated country which became Communist, or almost so.

The legal system of North Yemen is still basically a traditional Islamic system, operating along with the newly-promulgated statutory provisions. This country's legal system is in a state of development and the domains devised to traditional Islamic law and positive statutory law are ill-defined. It can be said, however, that most areas of modern economic activities such as international commerce, banking, foreign investment and energy law are governed by legislation whereas the traditional aspects of life such as family and inheritance remain Islamic in character.

In the field of economic development, South Yemen favours the monopoly of the State in all major economic sectors. All international trade is conducted by the State. The Government agencies have full control on imports and they supply the imported goods to the private sector. President Ali Naser Muhammad, who was deposed from presidency in the course of Civil War in January 1986, favoured economic liberalisation and more financial assistance from the conservative Arab States and the West. Although the Civil War was a power struggle between rival political personalities, as opposed to any ideological conflict, those who succeeded in the Civil War have shown themselves more committed to fundamental Marxist policies.

In line with the agrarian reform which abolished the feudal system, a unique development in South Yemen has been the organisation of small-scale labour in agriculture and fisheries, through workmen's, farmers and fishermen's cooperatives. All such cooperatives come under the general administrative supervision of the Department of Cooperatives in the Ministry of Agriculture and Agrarian Reform. The fishermen's cooperatives own, maintain and repair boats, engines, fishing gear and nets and make them available for use by members according to a set fee of 25% of catch for motorised boats and 10% for unmotorised.

At present throughout South Yemen, the small-scale, traditional fisheries are controlled and operated by cooperatives in all governorates except for a few remote villages in the sixth governorate. These cooperatives own most of the artisanal boats together with nets, engines and gear and allocate these for use by their members. In the fifth and sixth governorates, where roadway access is still very difficult, they also control marketing and distribution. There are at present fourteen or so fishermen's cooperatives, with a membership of 3,356 fishermen with associate members numbering about 3,000. The various types of traditional boats number about 1,532 including 640 one-man craft.

By contrast to the situation in the Democratic Yemen, the North Yemenies have adopted liberal free-trade and economic policies.

Indeed, in order to gain the confidence of the outside world, North Yemen has permitted foreign companies and financial institutions to operate inside the country. Furthermore, the Yemen Arab Republic allows for capital, profits and dividends to be freely transferred abroad, under Law No. 23 of 1975 which regulates domestic and overseas investment. Among the foreign banks permitted to operate in 1971 and 1972 were the Arab Bank, the British Bank of the Middle East, *Banque de l'Indochine,* Habib Bank, United Bank and, later in 1975, the Bank of Credit and Commerce International and the First National City Bank. Similarly foreign companies started to establish business relations with local merchants, some helping to finance local projects for the private sector.

We earlier referred to the South Yemen's attempts to improve the fishing industry, by organising the fishermen. In North Yemen, fisheries administration is included in the Agricultural Sector under the Ministry of Agriculture. Law No. 142 of 1972 created the legal framework for the establishment of a Department of Fisheries. This provided for the organisation, the regulation and development of fishing activities including conservation measures, the processing and marketing of fish and fish products, the formation of co-operatives, the collection and analysis of statistics, research, training of fishermen, and other related personnel, technical and administrative matters. So far, however, the post of Director General of Fisheries has not been permanently filled and most government fisheries activities remain at a low level.

By contrast to the situation in South Yemen, there are no significant commercial fishing enterprises in North Yemen. Nor are there any fishermen's organisations in North Yemen. Indeed no reliable fishery statistics are available but in 1976 production of fish was estimated to be about 13,000 tons; there are some 3,578 fishermen using 1,060 traditional boats based in about twenty villages around the coast with no facilities or roads. A revolving fund scheme to provide technical services, training and supervision to expand and imporve the present fleet has been created but not, it would seem, yet implemented. The above-mentioned situation shows that North Yemen – relying on the private sector – is less inclined to intervene in tradtional industries such as fisheries.

In addition to the socio-economic impact of the agrarian reform and fisheries' control which should result in greater economic benefits, South Yemen also provides all its citizens with some direct.

social services. These free services have many important differences from those north of the border, both in organisation and levels of provision, while South Yemen's system of health care is unique. As is to be expected from a Marxist-Lenninist State, South Yemen is committed to free national health care. It has attempted, with some success, to extend primary health services to the remote regions, as well as to train health personnel at a local level. This is to be contrasted with the situation in North Yemen where health care is dominated by the private sector. Indeed, there is a movement in North Yemen towards privatisation of part of tertiary health care – previously provided free of charge by the publicly-funded hospitals. Again while in South Yemen the government strictly controls drug and medical equipment imports, in North Yemen there is an unregulated booming market for the importation of pharmaceuticals. Thus in South Yemen the National Drug Company (which holds the monopoly for drug imports) controls the quality, quantity and cost of pharmaceuticals and artificial limbs. By contrast, in North Yemen the public sector (the Yemen Drug Company) imports less than a third of the total pharmaceuticals and medical equipments – leaving the bulk of the market to the private enterprise. This freedom has been abused particularly because North Yemen (unlike Kuwait and Saudi Arabia) does not impose adequate licensing restrictions and has introduced little quality control measures.

Another important issue is the women's right. As seen in Chapter 2, South Yemen has introduced legislation to emancipate South Yemeni women and the country's constitution pledges the equality between man and woman. The rate of female illiteracy in South Yemen (84 per cent of the whole female population) is an improvement compared with North Yemen where the rate of female illiteracy stands at 98 per cent. Similarly, while only 2 per cent of North Yemeni girls attend secondary schools, the rate in South Yemen is much higher, albiet a modest 11 per cent of the total number of the girl population who are of secondary school age. Another indicator of better provision of mother and child care in South Yemen is child mortality (children between 1-4 years). In North Yemen 39 per cent of all children born, die before the age of four. In South Yemen the rate has been reduced to 28 per cent. Generally, therefore, more and better social, health and education facilities are provided for women in South Yemen – compared with the situation in North Yemen.

To conclude therefore, it can be said that so far as social services and right to development is concerned, the citizens of South Yemen have faired slightly better than their cousins north of the border. This progress, however, as borne out in statistics, is very modest indeed. Furthermore, to assess the results of the two Yemens' progress, it is not enough to rely merely on quantity indices. In addition to these indices the local, social, tribal and traditional features must be taken into account to see whether these traditional patterns cater for the needs of the population either in full or in part. By way of example, the religious taxation (*zakat*) is given by the faithful to the poor quite independently from government apparatus. Such traditional institutions may well provide a very real social service to the poor and deprived – but such services will not find their way into government statistics. Similarly, many people may afford their children some elementary education in the form of Qur'anic schooling – run outside the State-maintained educational sector. Again their number will remain outside the government statistics for education which is based on State school's registers. Thus one must find out whether there have been any changes at all in these customary patterns, and if so to what extent. Unquantifiable changes, as well as the normal methods for measuring economic and social progress, must be monitored to afford an opportunity for formulating objective criteria for comparing the paths of development on a scientific basis in the two Yemens.

In terms of their aspiration for economic development, political and cultural independence, the changes in social, educational and legal norms are probably more signigicant than mere political and economic factors. Indeed the totally different experiences of the two Yemens can be an ideal comparative evidence to identify which line of policy brings better and more efficient results in terms of social and economic development and progress in developing countries. The study in this book has been mainly concerned with the development of the legal system, the administration of national and local government, the provision of social services and social justice in the two Yemens. A comparison of the two systems shows that progress has been pretty slow in both countries to date, while the future in both Yemens seems much brighter. The Marxist regime in the South, however, has provided better and more social services. Nevertheless, it has not achieved a satisfactory degree of either political cohesion or social progress. This in spite of the hardship which South Yemen has imposed on the upper-income sector of its population over the past two decades – many of whom have migrated to North Yemen. The situation in North Yemen which has adapted the free-market policy for its development is not much better. Smuggling and profiteering as well as bribery and corruption in the judiciary and civil service – is prevailing. The country has not been able to overcome its serious economic problems, and remains the second poorest country in the Middle East (South Yemen being the poorest of them all).

Specific Issues

We have already discussed, in a comparative context, various issues relative to law and justice in the two Yemens. There are a number of theoretical and descriptive issues of law which merit further discussion in this context. We shall highlight these points in the following pages before making a final conclusion as to the nature and scope of legal development in the two Yemens.

The Position of Islamic Law

As discussed in chapters 2 and 3 there are formal acknowledgements within both the North and South Yemeni constitutions as to the supremacy of Islamic law as the State religion and as a source of law. However, the legal developments occuring in both Yemens since their respective revolutions have been largely induced by the secular climate. In the course of legal reforms introduced immediately after revolution, the intellectual trends and political thought in both sides of Yemen were un-Islamic – if not anti-Islamic. These trends were the same as those prevailing in other parts of the 'progressive' Arab world – mainly Egypt. South Yemen later broke with Islamic traditions altogether, choosing Marxist-Leninism as the foundation of its political thought and legal philosophy. In spite of some traces of Islamic law in recent legal developments in South Yemen – such as those dealing with family law, personal status and inheritance – one can conclude that this country is now developing its own brand of socialist law at the expense of both the Shari'a and tribal customary law.

The position of Islamic law in North Yemen deserves more investigation. As is well known, the Islamic revival has been a very strong movement throughout the Mulsim world in the recent past. The Muslim Brotherhood in Egypt, established by Hassan al-Banna (1906-1949), had a modest following but gained considerable sympathy in various parts of the Arab world.

Equivalent movements to the Muslim Brotherhood (itself generally confined to the Arab world), were also current in non-Arab parts of the Muslim world.[1] For instance, in the Indian subcontinent, the Jama'at-e Islami (founded by Maulana Abul Ala Maudoodi, 1903-79) has consistently campaigned for the establishment of an Islamic State. The Pakistan of to-day was born with the hope that it would develop into an Islamic State. Since the establishment of the Islamic Republic of Iran, the Islamic movement has gathered greater momentum throughout the Muslim world. It is, therefore, surprising that North Yemen, which has had first hand experience of a form of Islamic government under the Imams of Yemen, has been very slow to call for an Islamic Republic. It may be that the corrupt and unpopular regime of the Imams has made the majority Muslims of North Yemen reluctant to revive the old system or anything resembling it. This is, in historical terms, ironic. In Pakistan, Iran and several other Muslim countries which have been campaigning most strongly for an Islamic State, Islam has not possessed a State of its own. By contrast in North Yemen and Turkey, the two Muslim countries with a nominal Islamic State, the political campaign has been for total abolition of their respective existing Islamic governments, and not for their modification and/or purification. The reason for this irony may be that the nature of political thought prevailing in North Yemen and Turkey has ceased to be Islamic. it has become secular, based primarily on such political European thoughts as nationalism and constitutionalism.

Since the Iranian revolution of 1978-79 the Western media have highlighted the revolutionary character of the Shi'i school of Islam, thus implying that orthodox Sunni Islam is void of such revolutionary essense. This is, of course, untrue as witnessed by history; on many occasions the opposite has been the case. A case in point is the Zaidi branch of the Shi'i school in North Yemen. The Zaidis are named after Zaid (a grandson of the Third Shi'a Imam, Hussein, d.680) who rebelled against the Ummayed dynasty and was slain in 740 AD at Kufa (Iraq). He is revered as a religious and political martyr by all branches of Shi'i Islam. However, while Imam Muhammad Baqir (d. 731 AD), recognised as the fifth Imam by the majority of Shi'a (the Twelvers), did not seek confrontation

---

1. For a good account of the theoretical bases of an Islamis State see NOORI, Yahya and AMIN, S.H., *Legal and Political Structure of an Islamic State: The Implications for Iran and Pakistan,* Glasgow: Royston Ltd, 1987.

FAMILY TREE

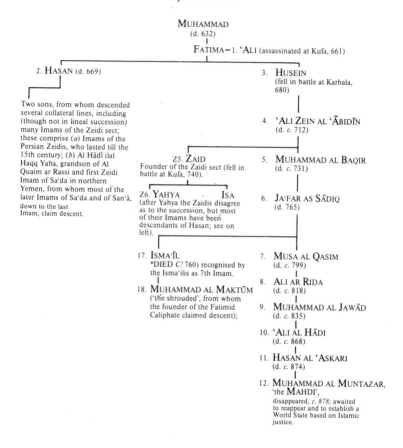

MUHAMMAD
(d. 632)

FATIMA = 1. 'ALI (assassinated at Kufa, 661)

2. HASAN (d. 669)

3. HUSEIN
(fell in battle at Karbala, 680)

Two sons, from whom descended several collateral lines, including (though not in lineal succession) many Imams of the Zeidi sect; these comprise (a) Imams of the Persian Zeidis, who lasted till the 15th century; (b) Al Hādī ilal Haqq Yaha, grandson of Al Quaim ar Rassi and first Zeidi Imam of Sa'da in northern Yemen, from whom most of the later Imams of Sa'da and of San'ā, down to the last Imam, claim descent.

4. 'ALI ZEIN AL 'ĀBIDĪN
(d. c. 712)

Z5. ZAID
Founder of the Zaidi sect (fell in battle at Kufa, 740).

5. MUHAMMAD AL BAQIR
(d. c. 731)

Z6. YAHYA   ISA
(after Yahya the Zaidis disagree as to the succession, but most of their Imams have been descendants of Hasan; see on left).

6. JA'FAR AS SĀDIQ
(d. 765)

17. ISMA'ĪL
*DIED C! 760) recognised by the Isma'ilis as 7th Imam.

18. MUHAMMAD AL MAKTŪM
('the shrouded', from whom the founder of the Fatimid Caliphate claimed descent);

7. MUSA AL QASIM
(d. c. 799)

8. ALI AR RIDA
(d. c. 818)

9. MUHAMMAD AL JAWĀD
(d. c. 835)

10. 'ALI AL HĀDI
(d. c. 868)

11. HASAN AL 'ASKARI
(d. c. 874)

12. MUHAMMAD AL MUNTAZAR,
'the MAHDI',
disappeared, c. 878; awaited to reappear and to establish a World State based on Islamic justice.

Pedigree[1] showing relationship of the several series of Shi'a Imams. The Ith na Asharis ('twelvers') recognise Nos. 1 to 12. The early Isma'ili Imams are numbered 1-6, I7, 18, the fist six being identical with those of the twelvers. The Zaidis also recognise Nos 1 to 4, after whom they recognise Zaid and his son Yahya; it is said that some Zaidis also recognised Yahya's brother Isa, but there is not complete agreement as to the succession of the later Imams, who form a long series, all selected from different branches of the House of 'Ali, but not all in lineal succession. Dates are in terms of the Christian era.

[1]Full pedigree in H. C. Kay, *Yaman, its Early Mediaeval History,* p. 302 (1892).
(Taken from *Western Arabia and the Red Sea,* London, 1946, p. 387).

94

with the State, Zaid openly led a revolt bidding for the leadership of the Muslim community.

The Zaidis believe that any member of the Ahl al-Bait (Family of the Prophet) who stands forth publicly and claims the office of Imamte i.e. the leadership of the *Umma* (Muslim Nation) should be recognised as Imam – provided that he is physically and spiritually competent to lead the *Umma*. Theoretically therefore, the Zaidis differ considerably from the Ja'fari school, religious leadership (Imamate) is an *exclusive* legacy, bequeathed from father to son. By contrast, in the Zaidi school, the leadership and governance of the *Umma* or Muslim Nation is selective and thus open to competition amongst the qualified descendants of the Prophet. The Zaidis are thus closer in both political thought and legal philosophy to Sunni Islam than to the majority Shi'i school.

We may consider further here the nature, character and substance of the constitutional structure of an Islamic State. Theoretically, in both Sunni and Shi'i schools sovereignty is vested in God. This Divine Sovereignty means that the State must submit to and obey God as the Divine Sovereign and supreme power. It also follows that no other person can claim sovereign rights over people. Indeed, even the Prophet Muhammad and his successors (whether as Caliph or Imam) did not possess sovereignty over Muslims. In an ideal Islamic State, both in theory and practice, the sovereign is God the Master of Man and the entire Universe. All Muslims should submit to His sovereignty. In practical terms this submission means that all human subjects must accept and obey the fixed and immutable principles of Devine Law in all aspects of their lives.[2]

Islamic law and constitution as the reflection of Divine revelation, exists in its own right. Put otherwise, Islamic legal and political principles are totally independent of the wishes and aspirations of the people. For Muslims, the right to legislate is, in general, the prerogative of God. Some minor and specific issues may be regulated by man-made subordinate legislation provided always that these secondary legislative acts conform to Islamic principles.

If the essense of Islamic governance i.e, sovereignty of God is

2. For details see the text of the author's lecture on "Islamic Law in the Contemporary World" delivered on 17th June 1986 at Fitzwilliam College, University of Cambridge. The text was published by the Islamic Academy, Cambridge, 1986.

realised, the form and style of government is immaterial. That is to say that the form of government can be either monarchical or republican, by selective appointment or elective in the form of general election. This is borne out in the history of early Islam. The first Caliph, Abu Bakr (d.632 AD) was elected; the second Caliph, Umar (d. 644 AD) was appointed by his predecessor; the third Caliph Uthman (d. 656 AD) was selected from amongst a number of nominees by a panel. The forth Sunni Caliph, Ali (d. 661 AD) came to power by popular demand. Thus none of the four rightly guided Caliphs succeeded their predecessor by the same rule of succession which applied to the others.

The Muslim Nation is styled as Ummah (i.e. the universal Muslim community without any geographical or political boundaries). It is to be organised, primarily, by reference to religious values and spiritual principles. Thus an Islamic State is totally different from the well-known Western and Eastern constitutional systems. The Islamic State has its own eternal rules, laws, morals, values, ideals, doctrinal dogmas, conditions and requirements. Its first fundamental principle relates to total obedience to the textual sources of the Qur'an and Sunnah in all affairs of the State and people. Another principle relates to the universality of Islam, both as faith and law. This implies that the Islamic State should ultimately extend to the whole of the globe and should encompass the whole of humanity. Finally, in the Islamic system of government, all persons, even the supreme leaders of the community are equal before the eternal principles of Islamic law. However, it should be emphasized that the Islamic form of government is not equivalent in theocrasy, at least according to Sunni schools of Islamic jurisprudence.

Amongst the Shi'a, some schools like the Zaidite consider the leadership (imamate) to be selective although the Imam must be chosen from amongst the descendants of the Prophet Muhammad. But to the Twelvers, when the Hidden Imam Mahdi appears he will be personally a representative of God. This amounts to a type of semi-theocrasy. Indeed the Inthna Ashari (Twelvers) Shi'i theosophy sometimes goes even beyond a mere semi-theocrasy. According to certain Shi'i traditions, compiled by collectors of hadith and selected by Mulla Sadra Shirazi, God did not create the Universe directly. He first made manifest the Universal Reason (aql-e koll) or the Prophetic Light (noor-e Muhammadi). This first creation was the Soul of the Prophet Muhammad and the Twelve Imams.[3]

The other significant branch of Shi'ism in North Yemen is that of Isma'ili, based in north and central yemen. The bulk of the Shi'a (namely the Ithna Ashariyah or Twelvers), believe in twelve Imams but the isma'ilis believe in seven. In spite of their belief in hereditary succession, the Twelvers acknowledge the power of theSixth Imam to pass over his elder son Isma'il and to nominate a younger son Musa. The Isma'ilis maintain that Isma'il, the eldest son, is the Seventh Shi'a Imam. The Isma'ilis themselves were divided into two groups. One group claimed that Isma'il was the promised Mahdi i.e. the last Imam of the Shi'a to reappear at the end of time. The other group acknowledged that Isma'il had died and thus believed the *Imamate* to continue through the progeny of his son Muhammad. The Isma'ili sect later grouped themselves together and began an organised political campaign in order to overthrow the Abbasid Sunni calihate and to establish a Shi'a caliphate instead. In or about 881 AD Ali ibn al-Fadl was sent to other parts of the Muslim world. Eventually the Isma'ili movement managed to establish a Fatimid caliphate in 899 AD. As there is no division between spiritual and temporal relams in Shi'ism, the new Fatimid Caliphate, based in North Africa, demanded obedience from all Muslims and formed a theocracy. Some factions of the Isma'ili sect – mostly based in Syria, Iraq, Persia and Bahrain – rejected the Fatimid proclamation for religious and political reasons. These dissidents were termed *'Qaramita'* (plural of *qirmeti*). Isma'ilis in Yemen for a while remained loyal to the central leadership of the Fatimid caliphate but later many refused the authority of the Fatimid caliphs. this drift between the Isma'ili community in Yemen remained until 1094 when in another succession crisis, all the Isma'ilis in Yemen were united in supporting Musta'li as Imam. Following another succession dispute in the 1130's, the Isma'ilis in Yemen supported a candidate known as al-Tayyib in opposition to another candidate in Egypt. Thus the Yemeni community became independent from the central authority in Egypt and survived while many other Isma'ili communities elsewhere disintegrated. This line of religious authority was maintained in certain Yemeni

3.   For details see AMIN, S.H., *The Philosophy of Mulla Sadra,* London, 1986, 6th edn., pp.181-190.

families until 1565 AD when the headquarters of the Isma'ili religion was transferred to India.[4]

The Isma'ilis had been protected by the local rulers in Yemen until the Zaidi Imams took power. The Isma'ilis suffered persecution and extirpation from the Imams of Yemen. Thus the Isma'ili community has dwindled to a smaller number in recent time.[5]

Economic Development

North Yemen sees the creation of a 'modern' legal system as an effective means to facilitate economic development. A legal system is thus being developed to serve modernisation and economic growth. This process has been enhanced as North Yemen has begun to enjoy the develolpment of its oil and gas resources – discovered by the Hunt Oil Co. in Ma'rib region close to South Yemen's border. The government of North Yemen has already set up a State-owned petroleum company – the Yemen Oil and Minerals Corporation (Yominco). The government has also granted exploration licenses for its vast offshore areas including some in northern Tihama. These exploration and exploitation activities will dominate the economic scene for the forseeable future. In the meantime the legal and administrative requirements of the oil and gas industry will have a significant impact on the field of law and administration in general. That is to say, if and when necessary other areas of law must be shaped in such a way that they would not conflict with the orderly and smooth development of these natural resources.

In July 1986, the Yemen Oil and Minerals Corporation, Yominco, borrowed two hundred million U.S. dollars from a group of mainly Arab banks to tide the country over until its oil reserves are exploited. The mere ability to obtain such a large loan commercially is convincing evidence that the capitalist world is now considering North Yemen as a nation with good economic prospects. In unison with this prospective affluence, North Yemen will continue to use the law as an instrument which would ensure the envisaged economic development.

4. POONAWALI, Ismail K., *Bibliography of Isma'ili Literature,* Malibu, California: Undena Publications, 1977, pp.4-10.

5. United Kingdom (Naval Intelligence Division), *Western Arabia and the Red Sea,* London, 1946, pp.388-389.

Once the North Yemen's own oil production starts, South Yemen will fall further behind the North in terms of material prosperity and economic progress. In the absence of oil, South Yemen must rest its hope on the development of its vast marine resources. However, it seems inevitable that the gap between the North and South Yemens will widen in economic terms in the post-oil era.

The oil and gas wealth will strengthen the role of central Government and will consolidate the State's power both domestically and internationally. Also the oil production will inevitably bring the North Yemeni government closer to the free world economic system via its contacts with the Western oil companies operating in its territory. Fascinated as it is by the prosperity which the oil wealth seems to promise, North Yemen may well decide to distance itself completely from the anti-Western sentiments which were popular during the republican movement.

The Nasserite ideology, strong during the revolution, has already changed not only in North Yemen but also in Egypt itself. North Yemen, influenced by the economic power of the American and or European oil companies will gradually move closer towards the Western Capitalist system. This will also be encouraged by Saudi Arabia and its allies in the Gulf Co-operation Council. Thus South Yemen will become more isolated and the vision of a United, conceived as a threat by Saudi Arabia, will become more remote.

If North Yemen is admitted to OPEC and OAPEC it will most probably follow an independent line on oil policy, basically reflecting its own national interest as a small producer. Thus while politically North Yemen will be supporting Saudi Arabia's policies, its oil policy may well be totally different given the different interests applying to a new small producer such as North Yemen and an established large producer such as Saudi Arabia.

North Yemen is hoping to develop its economy by collecting taxes – both directly and indirectly – from its larger and better off population. This country operates an 'open door' economic policy, aiming at attracting foreign investments. The main incentive provided by North Yemen for attracting such investments is a guarantee to pay total compensation to foreign investors in the event of nationalisation. This government guarantee will become more meaningful when the oil production in North Yemen places this country in a much more secure financial position. Another relevant issue is the provision for joint ventures in which the foreign participants may have a stake ranging from ten to ninty per cent of the total capital. This foreign share of the capital can be either in the form of cash contribution or by means of providing machinery, patents or trademarks.

The North Yemeni regulations for the registration, management and liquidation of domestic business ventures are still in the process of development. By contrast, there are clear regulations governing the foreign companies operating within this country. Any foreign natural or legal person wishing to do business in North Yemen must register with the Ministry of Economy, submitting a list of documents required by the Registrar of Foreign Corporations. In general, few foreign companies have opted for registering a branch in North Yemen as most of the business can be effectively handled by appointing agents. In terms of the Law of 6 December 1976, only Yemeni nationals and/or Yemeni-controlled companies can be employed as agents.

Except for pharmaceutical products and agricultural equipments which can be imported free of customs duties into North Yemen, all goods are subject to the Customs Co-operations Council Nomenclature (ex-Brussels). The rate of North Yemeni custom dues, however, differ from one category to another – ranging from 5 per cent to 145 per cent. The imposition of customes dues and taxes on imports form a sizeable portion of the State revenue. In point of fact, taxes and customs on international trade make up more than half of the total State income. This is, however, declining because the increasing industrialisation would mean more import substitution, thereby reducing government revenue from imports. it is also an open secret that as much as 25 per cent of the total imports into North Yemen remain undeclared for tax purposes. Most of this volume comes on major highways overland from duty free Saudi Arabia. It is through this route that millions of dollars' worth of goods slip across the international frontier every month. Modern North Yemen, with its liberal business law and practice, is a country with a huge black economy – both in imported goods and foreign hard currencies. South Yemen calls this situation a paradise for smugglers; North Yemenis may think their country offers more opportunities for enterprise. At the end, it is a matter of ideological orientation and economic culture.

Size of Population
The relatively small population of South Yemen (less than two million) in itself restricts this country's potential for economic development. This problem is further reinforced by the uneven spread of the population in different regions of South Yemen. The disparity between just one main urban centre (Aden) and the rest of the country, creates additional obstacles for future economic development in South Yemen. By contrast the smallish size of the population in this homogenous Sunni Arab communist country is an advantage in reaching concensus and in the process of forging a participatory society. North Yemen is less fortunate in this respect. Its population of more than nine million are divided into Shi'i Zaidis and Sunni Shafi'is. Hence it is more difficult here to achieve political concensus. On the other hand, this large population can participate in any appropriate programme for future economic development. Added to this advantage is the discovery of oil in North Yemen. Oil and gas will soon become the major economic base of this country.

In the course of exploration and exploitation of its on-shore and off-shore resources, North Yemen will be able ro provide employment opportunities for its own nationals. This may even attract many Yemenis currently working in the Gulf States to return home. In conclusion, the size of South Yemen's population is good for political reasons but not for economic development. By contrast the larger population of North Yemen is an advantage for the purposes of economic development but makes political cohesion less attainable.

Cultural and Social Attitudes
In terms of cultural and social attitudes as well as political and economic priorities, the South and North Yemens make odd partners. To the south lies the socialist stronghold looking up to the USSR, while to the north lies a country longing for an oil boom. The disparity of the two Yemens will become more evident when the North Yemen's oil production starts. This economic factor will be another obstacle towards possible unification of the two countries. Unification is not, and will not, be possible for the forseeable future, owing to the two Yemens' basic difference in political orientation and social structure. Thus while both countries wish to merge, each wishes to impose its own terms for union upon the other. South Yemen seeks to have a United Yemen committed

to international socialism. North Yemen wishes to bring about a united country allied with the conservative Arab world. Hence there is no concrete evidence that the mystical theory of union is achieving any success. By contrast, there is a good evidence that the two Yemens' differences are so deep-rooted that they end up in the open hostilities. For instance, South Yemen mounted a massive invasion of North Yemen in 1979. This was done in the hope that such external pressure would cause internal unrest and/or popular revolution to topple the government of North Yemen (not like the Iraq invasion of Iran a year and a half later in which Iraq hoped to bring Ayatollah Khomeini's rule in Tehran to an end). To these major problems, North Yemen's oil wealth will add a new dimension. The *Yemenis* to the North would not wish to share their newly-found fortune with any 'outsider'.

It is for the sake of this primary objective that South Yemen is trying hard to change the country's culture so that it would support the government imposed legal structure. This country's Ministry of Culture is systematically promoting the socialist culture. It also aims at a popularisation of national and socialistic Arab culture by fostering several unions such as the Union of Writers, the Union of Young Writers and the Union of Artists. The professional party officials also attempt to inform, encourage, educate and indoctrinate the younger generations so that they will develop a taste for the socialist system. South Yemen rejects the Arab nationalsit ideologies. Regarding both Nasserism and Ba'thism as *petit bourgeoisie,* the South Yemeni legal system is increasingly influenced by Socialist ideas and principles. By contrast, North Yemen immediately after its 1962 revolution, was very much influenced by the Egyptian legal traditions – particularly in areas of administrative and public law. In recent times, however, North Yemen, following a free market economic policy, has been gradually shifting away from the Nasserite Egyptian models. Impatiently awaiting the start of its oil wealth, North Yemen is lookin to the legal codes of Kuwait and Saudi Arabia for guidance and inspiration. At the same time the political influence of Saudi Arabia is bound to have some impact on the patterns of legal development in North Yemen. Saudi Arabia is suspicious of any progress towards unification of the two Yemens. North Yemen's legal and political institutions are now taking shape in such a fashion as would move this country's system away from the socialist patterns developed by South Yemen.

North Yemen has focused more on economic development and raising the standard of living of its nationals, implying that once the country is better off financially the social problems will be solved. Thus it would be the responsibility of people to compete for opportunities and then to obtain better housing, health care, education and other facilities through their own efforts. South Yemen takes it to be the responsibility of the State to provide these services and to control the economic and social changes directly. By way of example qat chewing, a significant feature of both Yemens' social and economic life, has been banned in South Yemen during the weekdays (Saturday to Thursday). This is because the Government of South Yemen wishes to guide its citizens, effect improvement of their social habits and eliminate health risks. Yet in North Yemen the consumption of qat has increased in recent years. The affluence resulting from larger remitted income from Yemeni workers abroad and generally more economic growth opportunities allow more people to indulge in spending time and money in qat parties. The chewing of qat gives the consumer a sense of well-being.[6] This relative affluence, real or imagined, has also resulted in an increase in alcohol consumption in spite of the Islamic prohibition of all alcoholic substances.

Legal System

So far as the development of the legal system is concerned, both Yemens have witnessed a sharp increase in legislative enactments and government regulations since their respective revolutions. In North Yemen these new laws concentrate on the economic and fiscal sectors. These regulate mining and quarrying; industrial manufacture; import and export; energy, oil, and electricity; transport and communications; business organisations and company regulations; service industries including banking, insurance and stock-related activities; foreign investment and joint commercial ventures. By contrast the radical South Yemen has embarked upon a socialist course. Accordingly the State is empowered to take charge of South Yemen's economic and financial planning and management. The State is in control of all the major means of production, whereas small farmers and fishermen are encouraged to organise co-operatives and participate

6. WEIR, S., *Qat in Yemen,* London: British Museum, 1985.

in trade unions. Furthermore, South Yemen has been trying to influence the nation's social and cultural values and behaviour through a new criminal code. Most of these legislative innovations and legal reforms reflect the ideological and political influence of the USSR. However, the revolutionary regime inevitably had to take note of the Islamic Shari'a in various areas of law, particularly those connected with family, personal status and criminal law. But even then the government had introduced a degree of reform to bring the legislation closer to the State's ideological perceptions.[7]

Notion of Property and Pricvate Enterprise
In terms of economic development, South Yemen is fully committed to collectivism and socialist economic patterns, thereby restricting private enterprise and speculative gain. Not surprisingly, therefore, the concept of property ownership in South Yemen does not correspond to the notion of private ownership in the capitalist North Yemeni system. To begin with, South Yemen is biased towards State ownership. The revolutionary regime has nationalised residential properties in towns. The State also dominates farming. Already up to six per cent of the country's cultivated land, confiscated from large landlords and religious endowments, is directly vested in the State. These are farmed by agricultural labourers who are simply paid fixed wages by the Ministry of Agriculture and Agrarian Reform. The bulk of the agricultural lands are farmed by farmers' co-operatives. Some 45 co-operatives hold about seventy per cent of the agricultural land. Thus less than a quarter of the country's agricultural land is farmed by private landlords. The independent farmers' holding, however, is, in terms of the Agrarian Reform Law of 1970, limited to a maximum of 21 acres for individuals and nuclear families and to 42 acres for extended families.[8] Such limitations to property ownership do not exist in North Yemen.[9]

Communist activities are outlawed in North Yemen although

---

7. See for example the discussion on Women's Rights and in particular the abolition of polygamy.

8. This limit is far more than the maximum ownership allowed in Afghanistan, the only other Muslim country with a Communist regime. The Land Reform Decree of 1978 fixed maximum agricultural holding in Afghanistan at 14.82 acres. For details, see AMIN, S.H., *Middle East Legal Systems,* Glasgow: Royston, 1985, pp.3-15.

9. For details, see ZIADEH, F., *Property Law in the Arab World,* London, 1979.

communist movements have been aggressive in the Arab world. There are established communist parties in a number of Arab countries including Syria, Iraq and Lebanon. However, amongst the Muslim countries, only South Yemen and Afghanistan have governing communist parties, directly based on Soviet models and patterns. Several other socialist Arab States, e.g. Algeria, Iraq and Syria have adopted a socialist system., albeit they label it Pan-Arabism, Ba'thism or nationalistic socialism. These countries attempt to interpret the Islamic Shari'a and the Arab tribal traditions as favouring socialism. By contrast, North Yemen and the conservative Arab States, led by Saudia Arabia, preclude and interference in private ownership, again with reference to the Islamic legal principles.

Human Rights
Under the contemporary rules of public international law (the U.N. Charter of 1945 and the Universal Declaration of Human Rights of 1948 etc.) it is acknowledged that every individual has the same minimum fundamental rights – irrespective of the political, cultural and religious system to which he belongs. Saudi Arabia and post-revolutionary Iran as well as a number of other Muslim countries have stated that the Muslim nations should be allowed to abide by the provisions of Islamic law which, to Muslims, must run supreme to any other legal framework.

It is undeniable that Islamic law provides considerable respect and protection for human life and human rights. Its provisions, however, do conflict, in certain respects, with the international law of human rights. Such areas of conflict can be seen in cases of women's rights and rights of non-Muslims. In addition to these basic issues, there is the often *de facto* discrimination against Muslims of minority schools. Thus in North Yemen where the Zaidi shi'i sect is the majority, the Sunni Sahfi'is and the Isma'ili Shi'is have both suffered discrimination under the Imams of Yemen. At present there is a kind of compromise between the two main Shi'a and Sunni communities in North Yemen with the balance of power favouring the Zaidis. By contrast, in South Yemen with its homogenous Sunni population, the other minorities will be at a relative disadvantage.[10]

Women's Rights

The Qur'an states that: "Men are the protectors and maintainers of women . . ." (Chapter 4, verse 34). This verse has traditionally been interpreted as giving man superiority over the women. This is further emphasised by the rest of this verse which says: ". . . because Allah has given the one more (strength) than the other, and because they support them from their means. Therefore the righteous women are devoutly obedient, and guard in (the husband's) absence what Allah would have them guard . . ." More importantly, the Qur'an states that men are *quwwamuna ala al-nisa*, which means that men are guardians over, protectors and maintainers of, or responsible for women. In another place the Qur'an states that: ". . . Any women shall have rights similar to the rights against them, according to what is equitable; but men have a degree (of advantage) over them and Allah is Exalted in Power" (Chapter 2, verse 228). These Qur'anic pronouncements are generally taken by Muslims as the religious foundation for the current domination and superiority of men over women in the Muslim world. There are also some specific rules of law mentioned in the Qur'an which treat women less favourably than men. For instance in bearing witness in certain matters the Qur'an states:

". . . And get two witness, out of your own men, and if there are not two men, then a man and two women, such as ye choose, for witnesses, so that if one of them errs, the other can remind her. . ." (Chapter 2, verse 282).

This policy of considering the testimony of two women equal to that of one man is a specific rule but nevertheless reflects the lower status of women before official authorities. In addition to this, it is universally acknowledged by all schools of Islamic law that the right to leadership (imamate or caliphate) in Islam is confined to the male sex. In areas of private law so far as discrimination against women is concerned the Islamic law of inheritance, divorce and polygamy are the other main areas in which women's rights under

---

10. Such religious discrimination would seem strange in a socialist system which is theoretically hostile to all types of religion and thus must be in practice indifferent to various forms of it. However, a recent report coming out of Afghanistan shows that the Communist regime of Babrak Karmal while attempting to win the support of Sunni *ulama, has kept the Shi'a madrasas* closed. See, *Human Rights in Afghanistan since the Invasion 1979,* Helsinki Watch Report, December 1984. p.116.

Islamic law are violated by the contemporary standards of human rights. A husband has an absolute and exclusive right to divorce his wife at his sole discretion. He also has the unrestricted right to marry up to four permanent wives concurrently. These rights are unfettered by the 1978 legislation on family law in North Yemen. By contrast, South Yemen has modified them. The Personal Status Law of South Yemen, promulgated in 1971, was based on the Syrian Personal Status Law of 1953. It did not contest the husband's right to divorce and polygamy, but simply sought to regulate the financial aspects of these problems. The 1971 legislation, however, was repealed by the 1974 Family Law. This new law, based on the Tunisian Personal Status Law of 1959, makes divorce in South Yemen subject to a petition presented to the court of law by either husband or wife.

The recognition of polygamy in Islamic law is a legacy of the pre-Islamic customary law of Arabia. Then the typical Arab used to exercise his natural right to unrestricted polygamy; marrying a countless number of wives. These numerous wives were often treated unjustly, sometimes regarded by their husband as no more than cattle; some of them were absolutely neglected, as they became neither wives nor divorced, but just in between. Islam restricted the right to polygamy to a maximum of four wives. Islam recognised polygamy but did not recommend it and made it dependent on whether man is able to deal justly with more than one wife or not. If he is not able to do so, he must be restricted to one only. The Qur'an thus states:

"... Marry women of your choice, two or three, or four; but if ye fear that ye shall not be able to deal justly (with them), then only one, ...".

This commandment to deal justly with wives has been traditionally considered as a moral recommendation – not a legal requirement. Only in the twentieth century has this verse been interpreted by some 'enlightened scholars' as a legal condition without which the right to polygamy may not be exercised. Polygamy is now formally abolished in South Yemen, similar to the situation in Tunisia.[11] By contrast, the 1978 Family Law of North Yemen expressly confirms the right of a man to take four wives. The

11. For an early discussion of the Tunisian law reform as to the prohibition of polygamy, see COULSON, N.J., Islamic Law, in DERRETT, J.D.M., An Introduction to Legal Systems, London, 1968, pp.75-76.

North Yemeni law, however, disapproves of temporary marriage, a legal institution acknowledged by the Ja'fari Shi'a school (and prevailing in post-revolutionary Iran).

Finally, the law of inheritance also discriminates against women. They are discriminated against first of all because a son has twice as much right in his parents' estate as a daughter. Secondly, in Sunni law a daughter of the deceased does not exclude from succession any male agnate collateral relative. Thus Shi'i law which provides for this exclusion has been adopted by a number of Sunni – populated countries such as Tunisia so that now daughters have absolute priority in succession over the brothers of more distant agnate relatives of the deceased. In the Yemens where the concept of the tribal unit and male domination is still prevalent, the orthodox Sunni law of inheritance remains in force.[12]

How to Sustain Legal Reform

Whatever course for legal development is adopted, for any law reform to succeed there must be appropriate political, cultural, social and economic support. Without such complimentary developments, the law reform will collapse. The law will be reduced to a formal legal prescription printed in the official gazette (*de jure*), but totally void of any *de facto* impact on people's lives and behaviour. For example, if the age of majority is raised by legislation without providing an economic environment which can support the poor, most families will remain eager to marry off their daughters as soon as possible.

In North Yemen the victorious republicans stopped in 1962 the use of leg irons for convicts and abolished the holding of representative hostages by the central government – two of the notorious government practices under the Imams of Yemen.[13] Soon after the abolition, however, both practices had to be brought back, to the embarrassment of the post-revolutionary regime. Both these practices were found necessary in the North Yemeni political environment. The republicans realised that if these medieval institutions were not used, the new regime could not survive. Without such brutal practices, the revolutionary government in

12. COULSON, op cit, pp.77-78.

13. By holding hostages (often little boys between 5 and 11) from every tribal area in North Yemen, the central government maintained rigid control over all. For details, see UK, Naval Intelligence Division, *Western Arabia and the Red Sea,* London, 1946, pp.338-339.

108

North Yemen felt insecure. It feared for its own security and its ability to maintain public order.[14] A very similar situation occured in post-revolutionary Iran in connection with the abolition of the Shah's secret service SAVAK. The Iranian Constitution of 1979 expressly prohibited imprisonment without trial, torture, extra-judicial detention and any type of censor. But the post-revolutionary Iranian regime soon resorted to these forbidden practices. Indeed SAVAK was reorganised and all its previous activities revived a year or two after the 1979 revolution.[15] The reason for this unhappy experience in Iran is the fact that the new regime – like its predecessor – did not wish to allow any political participation to its opponents.

General Conclusions

Law and regulations must be viewed both as effects and causes of social and economic changes. National law is not a set of static rules and standards. The modern Yemeni States, both to the north and south, have attempted to use the law as a vehicle for changing regular patterns of behaviour whereby enforcing a new code designed to support the State-backed legal and political order. South Yemen by opting for public ownership of all the major means of production has placed a greater role on the State to realise social change and economic development. The law therefore is seen as having a 'functional role' in South Yemen – it must ideally work towards building up a collective and institutionalised political, legal and economic order developed by popular participation. In practice, however, as seen in the Civil War of January 1986, the post-independence legal, political and economic order, has generated a new generation of elites who would do their utmost to free themselves from public accountability and collective restraints.

North Yemen having been kept out of the world economic and political system by the Imams of Yemen until 1963, is keen to integrate into the Western-dominated free market. Aiming at modernisation and economic development, this country is creating a codified legal system patterned on the European legal structure.

14. STOOKEY, R.W., *The Arabian Peninsula,* Hoover Press Publications, 1984, p.XIV.

15. The Iranian parliament (Islamic Consultative Assembly – Majlis) approved a law establishing a Ministry of State Security and Intelligence in 1982. The name of the new ministry is identical to that of Savak except that the word 'ministry' is substituted for 'organisation'.

North Yemen hopes that the local traditions and tribal norms and religious values can give way to unitary legal standards introduced by the State. It plans to apply the secular law universally throughout the country so that they supercede the existing tribal and religious norms, institutions and practices. This, the government hopes, can be achieved by a process of economic development and political integration. South Yemen, true to its socialist values, charges that the economic development advocated by North Yemen would benefit only a relatively small section of the population – those who can act as agents, intermediaries and servants to foreign companies in the private sector and the administrators of the political economy of development in the public sector. It is argued, therefore, that the masses of people living in rural and tribal settings, termed 'backward and primitive', will be left out. Thus South Yemen, while it accepts the notion of a planned economy, emphasises the role of the State as the basic authority for an equal distribution of resources and delivery of services.

The opposing development of national laws in the two Yemens present an interesting case of comparative law. Both a descriptive and a theoretical comparison of the laws of these two sister States provide evidence of how and why law is used by these developing countries as an instrument for changing existing political, social and economic patterns. South Yemen uses the law for ensuring the social ownership of the means of production and for creating a corresponding socialist order. North Yemen is developing its national law to benefit better and more from the expansion of a free market economy based on private ownership of the means of production, the attraction of foreign investment and the growth of private enterprise. The law is used as the means for achieving these basically different aims. Neither country has had an absolute success in achieving its economic and social aims through law. This is further emphasised by the fact that in areas of private law, irrespective of the legal standards and patterns prescribed by the State, Yemenis on both sides of the border follow their traditional and tribal norms, values and practices. In other words the *de facto* regime remains mainly independent of *de jure*. In areas of public law, however, there is good evidence of a degree of success in the process of nation building. However, North Yemen owes its nationhood and independent status to the pre-revolution government of the Imams of Yemen. South Yemen has managed to incorporate its various population into a pan-tribal State but, as the events of the Civil War of 1986 proved, the tribal loyalties have not been completely superceded by duty to State and loyalty to party.

In South Yemen, the first major source of law is the Constitution of 1970 as amended on 31 October 1978. The Constitution does not adhere to the notion of separation of powers – legislative, executive, and judiciary. Instead sovereignty is vested collectively in "the working people" (Articles 62 and 68 of the 1970 Constitution). The second major source of law is secular legislation. South Yemen has promulgated several laws such as Family Law of 5 January 1974, Penal Code of 9 March 1976, Labour Law of 30 April 1978, Social Security Law of 28 April 1980, Court Law of 1 September 1980 and the Civil Code of 1983. These constitutional and legal frameworks are all designed to facilitate the transformation of the society and State into modern Socialist patterns. As such, South Yemen is a member of the Socialist legal systems. By contrast, North Yemen until few years ago was considered as a member of the Islamic family of legal systems. Indeed, North Yemen was one of the strongest candidates for being regarded a 'pure' Islamic legal system because it has not been directly influenced by colonial legislation in the past. All legal reforms introduced in the post-revolutionary era to the North Yemeni environment, has been the choice of the government; not the dictate of colonial masters. It is clear that North Yemen has chosen not to rely on its Islamic legal traditions. This country has now joined the modernist – reformist group among the Muslim nations for its future legal development.

The current legal trends in North Yemen are remarkable – given the legal, economic and educational institutions of the pre-revolutionary Yemeni Imamate. This country's secularist regime seems little affected by the international Islamic movements prevailing in various parts of the Muslim world. Under some pressure, the Permanent Constitution of 1970 emphasised the State's commitment to follow Islamic principles. In practice, however, the Ministers and government officials have been more inclined to follow secular and modernist policies. Within less than two decades, such important Islamic institutions as taxation, education and judiciary have been transformed into secular institutions. The secularists and advocates of reform in North Yemen, wish to follow the policies of the more developed Arab and European countries. However, compared with South Yemen whose militant socialist regime aspires to enhance secularism, North Yemen has retained much of its traditional legal culture.

Having a pre-capitalist economy, the two Yemens are amongst the poorest countries in the world both in terms of per capital income and of gross national product. In the South, the State intervenes in all aspects of life, introducing legal, economic and social reform against a background of colonialism and tribalism. Direct government control of economic activity has been periodically relaxed, but the overall dogmatic resolve of the Marxist regime to enforce collectivisation and worker participation is unshaken. The government is keen to promote the various sectors of its economy within a socialist legal and economic framework. As the only oil-poor Arab country in the region, PDRY's interest in oil exploration both offshore and onshore has increased. With more than forty per cent of its population employed in agriculture and fisheries, the government is committed to developing this sector by nationalisation, agrarian refom and the establishment of State farms. Out of some thirty State-owned farms, only half are profitable. So there is a growing emphasis on promoting private farming and fisheries through farmers' and fishermen's cooperatives. The fishing industry is a potential source of prosperity and exports in this sector were valued at 5.5 million dinars for the 1986 alone.

North Yemen has adopted a *laissez-faire* attitude towards economic activity and social change. This is evident in North Yemen's legal and business environment which is intended to encourage foreign investment and private enterprise. With better resources, North Yemen has been able to create a better infrastructure by developing communications and constructing highways compared with South Yemen. Not unlike the pre-revolutionary Iran, North Yemen is planning to develop its 'mother' or 'feeder' industries in the public sector in order to produce goods as inputs for pther products. The establishment of oil refineries, perto-chemical industries and fertiliser plants, are steps taken in this direction.

However one may view the objective and the function of the law, its interaction with economic realities cannot be overlooked. Both Yemens are making use of State law in order to create a legal environment suitable for their chosen road to economic modernisation and political innovation. Intending to reforn their existing institutions, the two Yemens are determined to break with their traditional and religious past and establish a completely secular system of law and government. This is remarkable because so many other Muslim countries in the 1970's and 1980's support a return to their roots in Islamic law and culture.

APPENDIX 1

THE 'AUDHALI CODE OF CUSTOMARY LAW*

The following is a free translation giving the substance of a treaty, based on tribal customary law *('urf),* made between the 'Audhali tribesmen and their own Sultan.

Private settlement of disputes

(1) Any dispute may be settled by a voluntary peacemaker, without fee. He shall separate the parties, and whoever resists shall incur the customary penalty. After a week's interval he shall proceed to a settlement. If a tribesman involved in the dispute demands to see the record of the customary law, no order of the Sultan can prevent him.

Arrest and trial of offenders

(2) (a) An accused tribesman who is tried by the Sultan shall be judged by customary law. The summons shall be a thread from the fringe of the Sultan's kilt. Should the accused fail to appear within three days he shall incur a fine of one dollar; provided that in the case of sickness or absence such period shall run from the date of his recovery or return. He shall also be liable to arrest but may be released upon giving up his dagger as bail for his appearance in Court. In default of arrest, or of appearance after having given bail, his ox shall be attached until he surrender.

Compensation for bloodshed

(b) A wound shall be kept under observation for the period of one year and the Sultan shall order a just compensation according to the nature of the wound. No compensation shall be paid for a trivial injury.

The Sultan's dues

(3) (a) The Sultan shall be entitled to receive hospitality when he requires it, and 'coffee money' (usually a sheep) on the occasion of a marriage or circumcision in his family, or on the 'demise of the crown'. He is also entitled to free entertainment, or a sheep in lieu thereof, when he visits a *locus,* e.g. in connection with a boundary dispute.

---

* First produced in *Geographical Handbook Series: Western Arabia and the Red Sea,* London: British Naval Intelligence Division, 1946, pp.587-589.

Debts due to the Sultan
(b) A debtor to the Sultan, whose field has been sequestrated, may release it by pawning his person or his ox, and he may release his ox by pawning his rifle.

Liability of shepherd
(4) (a) If a shepherd throw stones, to keep his flock from straying, he is liable in compensation to the owner if he hit and kill a sheep at the rear of the flock.

Sequestration of stock
(b).Neither cattle nor the camels which are used in irrigation shall be attached during the breeding-season.

Garrisoning of Laudar
(5) The Bijeiris shall supply two-thirds of the garrison of Laudar and the Tuheifis one-third. The garrison shall be exempt from legal process and from market dues on purchases but shall pay market dues of one-eighth of the price on sales.

Tribal feuds
(6) (a) Feuds between the tribes of the 'Audhali conferderation shall be settled by the tribesmen. The Sultan shall not intervene unless to impose a year's truce on the application of one of the tribes. No tribesman may enter the market-place of a hostile tribe unless he be weak or poor. If he has already entered he may not be harmed at the Sunday market but shall depart on Monday.

'Protected persons'
(b) The Sultan may grant or refuse permission to 'protected persons' to remain in the district. A 'protected person' is a stranger who lives under the patronage and protection of a tribesman of upright character. The patron may intercede with the Sultan on behalf of his protégé, and the matter shall be decided according to customary law.

Debtors
(7) A tribesman summoned for debt shall be allowed a week's delay. Failing payment within the week he shall pay 30 riyāls to the Sultan (or 15 riyāls to a member of the Sultan's house) as Court fees.

(8) Tribesmen shall pay to the naqib one load of red grain, and, for each ox owned by the tribesman, half a measure of corn and one scoop of millet.

Officers' fees

(9) A guard shall receive a fee of half a riyāl for an arrest or the attachment of an ox, unless the defendant give up a rifle or dagger as bail for his appearance in Court. Nothing shall be payable (except *ex gratia*) for his services on missions connected with disputes about irrigation rights or boundary marks, or to investigate complaints.

Fines for breaches of the peace

(10) The fine for a breach of the peace is payabe to the person who separated the parties, or, failing this, to the Sultan.

Liability of camel-driver

(11) A camel-driver who uses a stick over a yard and a half long to drive the camel which works a well shall be responsible if the beast die.

Upkeep of well

(12) The Bijeiris shall be responsible for two-thirds of the upkeep of the well of Am Shubibiyah, and the Tuheifis for one-third. Any dispute between them shall be punishable with a fine of 70 cattle.

Offences committed on the Thira road

(13) Whoever is guilty of homicide on the Thira road (an ancient track, formerly paved, dating from pre-Islamic times, up the Kaur range beyond Al Kubeida) shall pay a fine of 70 cattle, and whosoever is guilty of theft on the said road shall pay four times the value of the stolen goods and four cows for sacrifice.[1]

Fines in kind

(14) If cattle stray off the road into crops the penalty is the fine of an ox; and the penalty for breaking into a house is also an ox.

---

1. The cows are sacrificed on the scene of the theft and the flesh distributed to the poor. Such customs are almost uncertainly relics of pre-Islamic rites.

E

Maintenance of post

(15) Two-thirds of the cost of entertainment at the post of Am Rasas shall be borne by the Bjieiris, and one-third by the Tuheifis.

Exemption of a Sayid family

(16) The house of 'Omar ibn Ahmed al Jifri shall be exempt from payment of tithes, entertainment charges, and market dues.[2]

This is the table of the customary law. Any amendment shall have reference to this document.

---

2. The ancestor of this house, of whom there are many in the Hadh-ramaut, settled in the 'Audhali country at Al Kubeida. The case is a good example of the privileged position of Sayids, who frequently act as professional peace-makers.

APPENDIX 2

MARINE ZONES IN THE DEMOCRATIC YEMEN

Act No. 45 of 1977 concerning the Territorial Sea, Exclusive Economic Zone, Continental Shelf and other Marine areas.

Section 1
Title and Definitions

Article 1. This act shall be known as "The Act of 1977 concerning the territorial sea, exclusive economic zone, continental shelf and other marine areas".

Article 2. For the purposes of the present Act, the following words and terms shall, except where otherwise indicated, have the meanings assigned to them below:

Republic	–	The People's Democratic Republic of Yemen;
Prime Minister	–	The Chairman of the Council of Ministers of the People's Democratic Republic of Yemen;
Coast	–	The continental and island coastlines of the People's Democratic Republic of Yemen facing the Gulf of Aden, the Bab El Mandab Strait, the Red Sea, the Arabian Sea and the Indian Ocean in accordance with the maps officially recognised by the Republic;
Island	–	A naturally formed area of land, surrounded on all sides by water, which is above the water level at high tide;
Internal waters	–	The waters on the side of baselines from which the territorial sea is measured extending towards both the continental and the island land territory of the Republic;

117

Continental shelf – The sea-bed and subsoil thereof extending beyond the territorial sea throughout the natural prolongation of the Republic's land territory to the outer limit of the continental margin, or to a distance of 200 nautical miles from the baselines from which the breadth of the territorial sea is measured where the outer edge of the continental margin does not extend to that distance;

Contiguos zone – An expanse of water beyond the territorial sea of the Republic and adjacent to it as defined in article II of the present Act;

Bay – Any indentation or inlet or fjord or creek in the coastline or land protrusion in the sea;

Low tide elevation – A naturally-formed area of land which is surrounded by and above water at low tide but submerged at high tide;

Pollution of the marine envornment – The introduction by man, directly or indirectly, of substances or energy into the marine environment resulting in such deleterious effects as harm to living resources, hazards to human health, hindrance to marine activities, including fishing and other legitimate uses of the sea, impairment of quality for use of sea water and reduction of amenities;

Nautical mile – One thousand eight hundred and fifty-two (1,852) metres.

Section II
The territorial sea and contiguous zone

Article 3. The territorial sea, its bed and subsoil thereof as well as the air space, above it are subject to the sovereignty of the Republic.

Article 4. The territorial sea extends beyond the internal waters to a distance of 12 nautical miles seaward, measured from the straight baseline or from the low-water line along the coast as marked on large-scale charts officially recognised by the Republic.

Article 5. The baselines from which the territorial sea of the Republic is measured shall be as follows:

(a) Where the coast is wholly open to the sea: lines drawn from the low-water mark along the coast;

(b) In the case of islands situated on atolls or of islands having fringing reefs: lines drawn seaward from the low-water line of the reef;

(c) In the case of a bay facing the sea: lines drawn from one end of the land at the entrance of the bay to the other;

(d) In the case of a port or harbour: lines drawn along the seaward side of outermost harbour installations or roadsteads and lines also drawn between the tips of these installations;

(e) Where there is a low-tide elevation at a distance not exceeding 12 nautical miles from the coast: lines drawn from the low-water on such elevations;

(f) In localities where the coastline is deeply indented, curved or cut into, or if there is a fringe of islands along the continental coast: straight baselines joining appropriate points.

Article 6. (a) Foreign ships shall enjoy the right of innocent passage through the territorial sea of the Republic. Such passage is innocent so long as it is not prejudicial to the security, integrity and independence of the Republic.

(b) Passage of a foreign ship or submarine or underwater vehicle shall not be deemed innocent if in the territorial sea it engages in any of the following activities:

1. Any threat or use of force against the sovereignty, territorial integrity or independence of the State;

2. Any exercise or practice of any kind;

3. Any act aimed at collecting information to the prejudice of the defence or security of the Republic;

4. The launching, landing or taking on board of any aircraft or

military device;

5. The embarking or disembarking of any currency, person or commodity contrary to the immigration, security, customs, fiscal or sanitary laws and regulations in force;

6. Any act of wilful and serious pollution prejudicial to human health, living resources or the marine environment;

7. Any act of exploration, exploitation, or drilling for renewable or non-renewable natural resources;

8. Any survey or research activities;

9. Any act aimed at interfering with any systems of communication or any other facilities, installations or equipment;

10. Any activity which is not related to passage or is designed as to hamper international navigation.

Article 7. (a) The entry of foreign warships, including submarines and other underwater vehicles into and their passage through the territorial sea shall be subject to prior authorization from the competent authorities in the Republic.

(b) Submarines and other underwater vehicles are required to navigate on the surface and to show their flag while passing through the territorial sea.

Article 8. Foreign nuclear-powered ships or ships carrying nuclear substances or any other radio-active substances or materials shall give the competent authorities in the republic prior notification of their entry into the passage through the territorial sea.

Article 9. The competent authorities shall have the right to take all necessary measures in the territorial sea to prevent passage which is not innocent as well as to suspend the admission of all or some foreign ships to specified areas of the territorial sea should the public interest so require, provided that such areas shall be specified in a prior notification.

Article 10. Foreign ships exercising the right of innocent passage in the territorial sea shall comply with the laws and regulations in effect in the Republic, as well as with the rules of international law and, in particular, such laws and regulations relating to transport and navigation.

Article 11. The outer limit of the contiguous zone shall be the line every point of which is at a distance of 24 nautical miles from the nearest point of the baseline referred to in article 4 above.

Article 12. The authorities of the Republic have the right to impose, in the contiguous zone, the control necessary to:

(a) Prevent any infringement of its security, customs, sanitary and fiscal laws and regulations within its territory or territorial sea;

(b) Punish infringement of the above laws and regulations whether committed within its territory or within its territorial sea.

Section III
The exclusive economic zone

Article 13. The Republic shall have an exclusive economic zone the breadth of which extends 200 nautical miles from the baseline used to measure the territorial sea referred to in article 4 of this Act.

Article 14. In the exclusive economic zone, including its sea-bed and subsoil and the superjacent water column, the Republic has:

(a) Exclusive sovereign rights for the purpose of conserving, exploring, exploiting and managing its renewable and non-renewable natural resources, including the production of energy from the waters, currents and winds;

(b) Exclusive rights and jursidiction with regard to the construction, repair, operation and use of artificial islands, installations, facilities and other structures necessary for the exploration and exploitation of the exclusive economic zone of the Republic;

(c) Exclusive jursidiction over the marine environment with regard to its preservation and protection and to the prevention, control and abatement of marine pollution, as well as to the authorization, regulation and control of scientific research;

(d) Other rights recognised in international law.

Article 15. Without prejudice to the rights pertaining to it, the Republic guarantees the freedom of navigation, overflight and laying of submarine cables and pipelines in its exclusive economic zone.

Section IV
The Continental Shelf

Article 16. The authorities of the Republic may, to the exclusion of others, in the continental shelf:

(a) Explore, exploit, manage and conserve its natural resources;

(b) Construct, maintain, operate and use artificial islands, installations, facilities and other structures necessary for the exploration and exploitation of the continental shelf of the Republic;

(c) Regulate, authorise and control scientific research;

(d) Preserve and protect the marine environment and control and abate marine pollution.

Section V
Marine Boundaries

Article 17. (a) The demarcation of marine boundaries between the Republic and any State with adjacent or opposite coasts shall be effected, with regard to the territorial sea, the contiguous zone, the exclusive economic zone and the continental shelf, by agreement with the State;

(b) Pending agreement on the demarcation of the marine boundaries, the limits of the territorial sea, the contiguous zone, the exclusive economic zone and the continental shelf between the Republic and any State with coasts adjacent or opposite to it, the coast of the Republic shall not be extended to more than the nearest points on the baseline from which the breadth of the territorial seas of both the Republic and the other State is measured.

Section VI
The Island Territory

Article 18. Each of the islands of the Republic shall have a territorial sea, contiguous zone, exclusive economic zone and continental shelf of its own, and all provisions of this Act shall be applicable to it.

Section VII
General Provisions

Article 19. In exercising its sovereign rights and jurisdiction over the territorial sea, the exclusive economic zone and the continental shelf, the Republic shall have the right to take all necessary measures aimed at ensuring the implementation of its laws and regulations.

Article 20. Any foreign person, natural or juridical, shall be banned from exploring and exploiting the renewable and non-renewable natural resources of the territorial sea, exclusive economic zone and continental shelf of the Republic, from conducting any prospecting, drilling or search operations, undertaking any scientific research or prospecting drilling, construction or maintenance of any kind of artificial islands, stations (marine installations), devices or structures, or from conducting any operation or maintenance work for any purpose, unless he has entered into a special agreement with the Republic for this purpose or obtained a special permit from its competent authorities.

Article 21. Without prejudice to any more severe penalty laid down in any other law, any persons violating the provisions of this Act or the rules and regulations issued under it shall be subject to a penalty of not more than three years imprisonment or a fine of not more than 10,000 dinars. However, the court may also order confiscation.

Article 22. Any person causing any pollution detrimental to human helath or to the living resources of the marine environment in the internal waters, territorial sea or the exclusive economic zone of the Republic shall be punished with a prison sentence of not more than one year or with a fine of not more than 5,000 dinars.

Should such pollution result in serious harm, the penalty shall be a prison sentence of not more than three years or a fine not exceeding 10,000 dinars.

Article 23. The Prime Minister shall issue the decisions and regulations implementing and interpreting this Act.

Article 24. For the purposes of the present Act, any text which conflicts with its regulations, especially Act No. 8 of 1970 and Act No. 2 of 1972, shall be rescinded.

Press Communique of Muhammad Saleh Mute'i, Member of the Presidential Council and Minister of Foreign Affairs, Democratic Yemen, Aden 7 July 1978.

The Government of the People's Democratic Republic of Yemen is following the course of current development in our Arab area, which is witnessing efforts to expedite the implementation of the over-all imperialist design that is primarily aimed at liquidating the progressive national régime in our country and, consequently, the national régimes and national liberation movements in our area...

... Developments in this area cannot be separated from the comprehensive imperialist Zionist design which seeks to impede the growth and development of the people of the area and of its progressive national movements, and to reinstate and reinforce imperialist influence over it. Our Government is also fully convinced and has consistently shown, in its political and practical attitudes, that the proper method of solving any problems or differences that may arise among the peoples and States of the area, is one that is designed to avoid war, prevent recourse to violence and to observe peaceful means of settlement, through democratic dialogue and peaceful negotiations . . .

With regard to these numerous direct and indirect imperialist attempts, the Government of the People's Democratic Republic of Yemen has been paying attention to the Red Sea, not because it is one of the littoral States but also because it overlooks the southern entrance to the Red Sea and because it is fulfilling its international duties in connection with ensuring and protecting international navigation through the Sea. It has always declared in all Arab and international fora, in the consultative Ta'ez meeting and in the press communiqué issued by the two Yemens, that the red Sea should remain a zone of permanent peace and security and should not be subject to any foreign influence or domination. Our Government called, and is still calling, for co-operation among all States in the area to carry out this task and to exploit their resources, riches and sources of wealth for the benefit of their peoples.

Being well aware of the great importance of the Strait of Bab al-Mandeb to all peoples and States of the world as an international waterway which has long been used for international navigation, and of its important strategic location as a link between the international traffic lines, and believing in the importance of keeping international navigation through this vital strait free for the benefit of the peoples and States in the area in particular and the international community in general, the Government of the People's Democratic Republic of Yemen confirms its respect for the freedom of maritime and air trafficc of ships and aircraft of all coastal and non-coastal States, without prejudice to the sovereignty, integrity, security and independence of the Republic.

. . . In view of its concern for fruitful co-operation among the States and peoples of the area in the connection, the Government of the People's Democratic Republic of Yemen believes in the importance of rapprochement among all States of the area bordering on this vitally important waterway, and in the need for those States and peoples to follow the example of Democratic Yemen in ensuring freedom of maritime and air navigation for the benefit of all peoples of the world and in the interests of stability, peace, progress and development in various fields of life.

APPENDIX 3

Marine Zones In North Yemen

Territorial Waters (Decree No. 15, 1967)

Article 1. (Definitions of nautical mile, bay, island and so forth).

Article 2. The territorial waters of the Yemen Arab Republic, the air space over them and the land beneath them and the subsoil under them are under the sovereignty of the Republic, with due consideration of the rules of international law relating to the innocent passage of vessels of other nations in the coastal sea.

Article 3. The territorial waters of the Yemen Arab Republic include the inland waters and the coastal sea of the Republic.

Article 4. The inland waters of the Republic include:

(a) The waters of the bays along the coasts of the Republic.

(b) The waters above and landward from any shoal not more than twelve nautical miles from the mainland or from a Yemeni island, and the waters between such a shoal and the land.

(c) The waters between the mainland and any Yemeni island not more than twelve nautical miles from the mainland.

(d) The waters between the Yemeni islands which are not farther apart than twelve nautical miles.

Article 5. The coastal sea of the Yemen Arab Republic lies outside the inland waters of the Yemen Arab Republic and extends seaward for a distance of twelve nautical miles.

Article 6. The determination of the baselines from which the coastal sea of the Republic is measured shall be made according to the following:

(a) If the mainland or the shore of the island is fully exposed to the sea, the lowest low-water mark on the shore.

(b) In case of the existence of a shoal not more than twelve nautical miles from the mainland or from a Yemeni island, lines drawn from the mainland or the island and along the outer edge of the shoal.

(d) In case of the existence of a wharf or port facing the sea, lines drawn along the seaward side of the outermost works of the wharf or port and between such works.

(e) In case of the existence of an island not more than twelve miles from the mainland, lines drawn from the mainland along the

126

outer shores of the island.

(f)   In case of the existence of an island group which may be linked together by lines not more than twelve nautical miles long, lines drawn along the shore of all the islands of the group if the islands form a chain, or along the outer shores of the outermost islands of the group if the islands do not form a chain.

Article 7. If the measurement of the territorial waters in accordance with the provisions of this resolution leaves an area of high sea wholly surrounded by territorial waters and extending not more than twelve nautical miles in any direction, such area shall form part of the territorial waters. The same rule shall apply to a pronounced pocket of high sea which may be wholly enclosed by drawing a single straight line not more than twelve nautical miles long.

Article 8. In the event of waters of another State overlapping with the internal waters of the coastal sea of the Yemen Arab Republic the boundaries will be determined in agreement with the State concerned in accordance with the principles obsrved in international law or by mutual agreement.

Article 9. To enforce the laws and regulations relating to security, navigation, fiscal and sanitary purposes, maritime surveillance covers and area falling next to the coastal sea and contiguous to it, to a distance of six nautical miles in addition to the twelve nautical miles measured from the baselines of the coastal sea. This order shall not affect the rights of the Yemen Arab Republic with respect to fishing.

Continental Shelf (Decree No. 16, 1967)

Article 1. The Yemen Arab Republic enjoys sovereign rights over the sea bed and the subsoil of the continental shelf beyond the territorial waters of the Republic to a depth of 200 meters or, beyond the limit to where the depth admits of the exploitation of the natural resources which exist in the sea bed. The Yemen Arab Republic furthermore enjoys soveriegn rights over similar continental shelf in the case of islands belonging to the Yemen Arab Republic.

The foregoing do not affect the status of the superjacent waters of the said areas as being high seas or the freedom of navigation within the sea waters and in the air space above.

Article 2. The Yemen Arab Republic has alone the right of prospect, exploration and exploitation of all the natural mineral resources and other non-living resources together with living organisms belonging to sedentary species which exist on or under the sea bed of the regions mentioned in Article 1. To this end it has the right to construct, maintain and operate the installations necessary for this purpose, and to establish, for a distance of 500 meters around such installations, safety zones and to take in those zones measures necessary for their protection.

Article 3. The rights referred to in the two preceeding articles, or their exercise, do not depend on occupation, effective or notional, of the said regions or on any special declarations.

Article 4. It is forbidden for any foreign, natural or artificial, person to undertake the exploitation of any of the natural resources in the contintental shelf except be a decree from the President of the Republic.

BIBLIOGRAPHY

The bibliography is arranged in three sections. The first section lists the books and articles dealing with the contemporary Islamic and Middle Eastern law and justice, in general. The second section includes the material dealing with the South Yemeni political, constitutional and legal structure. The third section covers the material on North Yemen.

1. General Works

This section, listing books and articles on Islamic and Middle Eastern law in general, contains selected material published in European languages only. It is hoped that this will provide a useful and up to date reading list for further study of various aspects of law and justice in Islam.

ABDUL HALIM, Sh., *Muslim Family Laws,* Lahore, 1978.

ABDUR RAHIM, *Muhammadan Jurisprudence,* Lahore Tagore Law Lectures for 1907, reprinted 1963.

ABDUR RAHMAN, A. F. M., *Institutes of Muslim Law,* Calcutta, 1969.

ABU YUSUF, YAKOUB, *Kitab el – Kharadj,* translated as *Le Livre de l'impot Foncier* by Fagman, Paris, 1921.

ADAMS, C. C., *Islam and Modernism in Egypt,* London, 1933.

AGARWALA, K. S., "On the relative weight of the three Primary Authorities in the Hanafi School of Muhammedan Law", A. I. R. 1932 Journal 23.

AGNIDES, N. P., *Mohammedan Theories of Finance with an introduction to Mohammedan Law,* Lahore, 1961.

AHBAD, ABEL HAMID, L'arbitrage en Arabie Saoudite, *Revue de l'Arbitrage,* 1981, pp. 234-250.

AHMAD, M. B., *The Administration of Justice in Medieval India,* Aligarh, 1941.

AHMAD, M. B., "Theory and Practice of Law in Islam" (1961) 9 Journal Pakistan, Hist. Soc. 8.

AKHTAR, Shameem, An Inquiry into the Nature, Origin and Source of Islamic Law of Nations, 10 *Islamic Studies,* (1971), pp. 23-27.

AKHTAR, Shameem, Semantice of International Agreements by Early Islam, 6 *Islamic Studies,* (1967), pp. 81-95.

ALI, S. A., Law of Family Courts, Karachi, 1975.

AL – MARAYATI, A. A., *Middle Eastern Constitutions and Electoral Laws,* New York, 1961.

AL – MARGHINANI, Burhan al – Din, *The Hedaya* (or guide on Contemporary Muhammadian law), 2nd edition by S. G. Grady, London 1970. English translation by Charles Hamilton, *The Hedaya,* reprinted Lahore, 1963.

AL – MAWARDI, Abu al – Hassan, *Al – Ahkam al – Sultaniyya,* Cairo (nd), French translation and commentaries by D. Fagnan, Paris, 1915.

ÁLTMAN, I., "Islamic Legislation in Egypt in the 1970's" (1979) 13 Asian and African Studies 199.

AMEER, ALI SAYED, *Personal Law of the Mohammedans,* London, 1880.

AMEER, ALI SAYED, *Mohammedan Law,* Lahore 1976.

AMERDROZ, H. F., The Mazalim Jurisdiction in the Ahkam Sultanniyya of Mawardi, 2 *Journal of the Royal Asiatic Society,* (1911), pp. 635-674.

AMERDROZ, H. F., The Office of Kadi in the Ahkam Sultaniyya of Mawardi, 2 *Journal of the Royal Asiatic Society,* (1910), pp. 761-796).

AMIN, Sayed Alinaghi, *The Light of Truth,* Tehran: Vahid, 1986.

AMIN, Sayed Hassan, *Islamic Law in Public and Business Context,* Glasgow, 1986.

AMIN, Sayed Hassan, *Law of Justice in Muslim Africa,* Glasgow, 1986.

AMIN, Sayed Hassan, *International and Legal Problems of the Gulf,* London: Middle East and North African Studies Press, 1981.

AMIN, Sayed Hassan, *The Iraq-Iran War: Legal Implications,* London: Butterworth, 1982.

AMIN. Sayed Hassan, *Wrongful Appropriation and its Remedies in Islamic Law,* Glasgow, Royston, 1983.

AMIN, Sayed Hassan, *Islamic Banking and Finance,* Tehran, 1986.

AMIN, Sayed Hassan, *Remedies for Breach of Contract in Islamic and Iranian Law,* Glasgow: Royston, 1984.

AMIN, Sayed Hassan, *Middle East Legal Systems,* Glasgow: Royston, 1985.

AMIN, Sayed Hassan, *Islamic Law in the Contemporary World,* Tehran, 1985.

AMIR-SOLEIMANI, A., *La formation et les effets des contrats en droit iranien, compare avec le droit francais,* Paris thesis, 1936.

ANDERSON, J. N. D., *"Islamic Law in the Modern World"* London, 1959 (reprinted 1975).

ANDERSON, J. N. D., Sharia Today, in *Journal of Comparative Legislation,* London 1949.

ANDERSON J. N. D., *Islamic Law in Africa,* London 1955. (reprinted 1970).

ANDERSON, J. N. D., "Family Law in Africa and Asia" (London 1965).

ANDERSON, J. N. D., "The significance of Islamic Law in the World Today." (1960) 9 A. J. C. L. 187.

ANDERSON, J. N. D. in collaboration with N. J. Coulson, in "The Muslim Ruler and Contractual Obligations", *New York University Law Review,* November 1958.

ARCHIBALD, W. A. J., "Outlines of Indian Constitutional History", London, 1926.

ANSAY, Tugrel, et el, *Introduction to Turkish Law,* Ankara: Society of Comparative Law, 1978, 2nd. edition.

ARNOLD, Sir Thomas, *The Caliphate,* Oxford, 1924.

ARON, R., On Definition Clauses of some Oriental Deeds of Sale and Lease from Mesopotamia, 15 *Bibleithava Orientalis,* (1958), pp. 15-22.

.ASKARI, Hossein, CUMMINGS, John T., and GLOVER, Michael, *Taxation and Tax Policies in the Middle East,* London, Butterworth & Co. 1982.

BADR, G. M., "Islamic law: Its relation to other legal Systems". (1978) 26 A. J. C. L. 187.

BAILLIE, B. B. E., *The Mohammadan Law of Sale,* London, 1860.

BAILLIE, N. B. F., *Digest of Mohummudan Law,* London 1875.

BA'TH, M. H., *Islam Jurisprudence,* Washington, 1979.

de BELLEFONDS, Y. Linant, *Trait de droit musulman compare,* 3 volumes, Paris and La Haye, 1965, 1973.

BEN SHEMESH, A., *Taxation in Islam,* 3 volumes, Leiden 1965-1969.

BHATIA, H. S., *Origin and Development of Legal and Political system in India,* New Delhi, 1976.

BOUSQUET, G. H., *Le Droit Musulman,* Paris, 1963;

BOUSQUET, G. H., *Du droit musulman et de son application effective dans le monde,* Algiers 1949.

BRUNSHWIG, R., La preuve en droit musulman, 2 *Etudes d'Islamologie,* 1976, pp. 201-216.

BRUNSHWIG, R., Urbanisme medieval et droit musulman, 2 *Etudes d'Islamologie,* 1976 pp. 7-35.

AL-BUKHARI, Abu Abdullah Muhammad ibn Ismail, *Al-Jami al-Sahih* 9 volumes, Cairo. French translation by O. JHOUDAS and W. Marcais, Paris 1903-1904.

BUTLER, William and LEVASSEUR, George, *Human Rights and the Legal System in Iran,* (two reports) Geneva: The International Commission of Jurists, 1976.

130

BUZGHALIA, A., Le Litige international devant les tribunaux libyens, 4 *Dirasa Qanuyya,* (1974), Banghazi, pp. 35-95.

CALDER, N., Khums in Imami Shi'i jurisprudence, from the tenth to the sixteenth century A.D. *Bulletin of the School of Oriental and African Studies,* volume XLV, 1982, pp. 39-47.

CALDER, N., Zakat in Imami Shi'i jurisprudence from the tenth to the sixteenth century A.D. *Bulletin of the School of Oriental and African Studies,* volume XL1V, 1981, pp. 468-480.

CARDAHI, Chucri, Le conception et le pratique du droit international prive dans l'Islam, 2 *Recueil de Cours de l'Academie de Droit international de la Haye,* 1937, pp. 511-650.

CHAUDHARY, A. C., "Independence of the Judiciary and the Administration of Justice in Pakistan". Lawasia, 1972.

COULSON, N. J., "Muslim Custom and Case law," 1959 Welt des Islams 13.

COULSON, N. J., *A History of Islamic Law,* Edinburgh: (Islamic Surveys), 1964.

COULSON, N. J., *Conflict and Tensions in Islamic Jurisprudence,* Chicago, 1969.

COULSON, N. J., *Commercial Law in The Gulf States; the Islamic Legal Tradition,* London, Graham & Trotman, 1984.

COULSON N. J., Doctrine and practice in Islamic Law, *Bulletin of the School of Oriental and African Studies,* volume XV111 number 2, 1956, pp. 211-226.

DAURA, B., "A brief account of the Development of the Four Sunni Schools of Law and Some Recent Developments" 1968, J. I. C. L. 1.

DAVIS, Helen M., *Constitutions, Electoral laws, Treaties of States in the Near and Middle East,* Durham, North Carolina, 1947.

DEMOMBYNE, *Muslim Institutions,* London, 1950.

DERRETT, J. D. M., *An Introduction to Legal Systems,* London, 1968.

DJAMOUR, J., *Muslim Matrimonial Court in Singapore,* 1966.

DONALDSON, D. M., *The Shi'ite Religion,* London 1933.

DUBEY, H. P., *A short history of the Judicial Systems of India and Some Foreign Countries,* Bombay, 1968.

EISENMEN, R. H., *Islamic Law in Palestine and Israel,* Leiden, 1978.

EL-FALAHI, S. D., The legal environment for negotiating Commercial Agreements in the Middle East, *An Introduction to Business Law in the Middle east,* London 1975, pp. 75-87.

ENCYCLOPEDIA OF ISLAM, 1st edition, 4 volumes Leiden 1913-1942. 2nd edition, Leiden and London, 1960.

FARUKI, Kemal, *Islamic Jurisprudence,* Karachi 1962.

FARUKI, Kemal, *The Evolution of Islamic Constitutional Theory and Practice from 622 to 1926,* Lahore, 1971.

FATTAL, Antoine, *Le statut des non-musulmans en pays d'Islam,* Beirut, 1958.

FAWCETT, C., *The first century of British Justice in India,* Oxford, 1934.

FITZGERALD, S. G. V., Nature and Sources of the Shari'a, in Law in the Middle East, edited by M. Khadduri and H. J. Liebesny, Washington D. C. 1955.

FITZGERALD, S. G. V., The alleged debt of Islamic to Roman Law, 67 *Law Quarterly Review,* 1951, pp. 81-102.

FYZEE, A. A. A., *Outlines of Muhammadan Law,* 2nd edition, Oxford University Press, 1963. (4th edition, 1974).

FYZEE, A. A. A., *A Shi'ite Creed,* London, 1942.

FYZEE, A. A. A., "The Relevance of Muhammadan Law in the Twentieth Century" 1963 C. L. J. 261.

FYZEE, A. A. A., *Cases in the Muhammadan Law of India and Pakistan,* Oxford, 1965.

FYZEE, A. A. A., "The impact of English Law on Shari'at in India" 1964. 66 Bombay L. R. (J) 107, 121.

131

FYZEE, A. A. A., Development of Islamic Law in India-A bird's eye view." in *Sotio Cultural Impact of Islam on India,* ed. Attar Singh (Chandighar) 1976.

GHUNAIM, Mohammad Talaat, *The Muslim Conception of International Law and the Western Approach,* The Hague: Martinus Nijhoff, 1968.

GIBB, H. A. R., Some considerations on the Sunni Theory of the Caliphate, 3 *Achives d'histoire du droit oriental,* 1948, pp. 401-410.

GIBB, H. A. R., *Modern Times in Islam,* Chicago, 1947.

GIBB, H. A. R., *Whither Islam,* London, 1932.

GIBB and KRAMERS, *Shorter Encyclopedia of Islam,* Leiden, 1953.

GLEDHILL, A., "The reception of English Law in India" in W. B. HAMILTONS (ed) *The transfer of Institutions,* Durham N. C., 1964, p. 165.

GOLDZIHER, I., *Die Zahiriten,* Liepzig, 1884.

GOLDZIHER, I., *A short history of Arabic Literature,* (tr. Joseph de Somogyi), Hyderabad Deccan, n.d.

GOLDZIHER, I., *Muhammedanische Studien,* Halle, 1889.

GOLDZIHER, I., *Muslim Studies,* (translated by Barber, C. R. and Stern S. M.), London, 1971.

GUILLAUME, A., *The Life of Muhammad,* Oxford, 1955.

GUILLAUME, A., *The Traditions of Islam,* Oxford, 1924.

GUILLAUME, A., *Islam,* London, 1963.

HABASHY, Saba, Similarities and Common Principles of Western and Middle Eastern Systems of Law, 2 *Middle East Executive Reports,* 1979, pp. 2, 12-15.

HAJ NOUR, A. M., "The Schools of Law: their emergency and validity today" (1977) 7 J. I. C. L. 54.

HAMILTON, Charles, *The Hedaya,* London 1870 (see AL-MARGHINANI, suppra.)

HAMILTON, Charles, (ed. Grady) *The Hedaya,* London, 1870.

HASAN, Ahmad, *The Early Development of Islamic Jurisprudence,* Islamabad, 1970.

HASAN, Ahmad, "Al Shafi'i's Role in the Development of Islamic Jurisprudence", (1966) 5 *Islamic Studies* 239.

HASAN, Ahmad, "Ijma in the early Schools" (1967) 6 *Islamic Studies* 121.

HASAN, Ahmad, "Origins of the Early Schools of law" (1970) 9 *Islamic Studies* 255.

HASAN, Ahmad, "Modern Trends in Ijma" (1973) 12 *Islamic Studies* 121.

HASAN, Ahmad, The Principle of Istishan in Islamic Jurisprudence", (1977) 16 *Islamic Studies* 347.

HASAN, Ahmad, "The Theory of Naskh," (1965) 4 *Islamic Studies* 181.

HASAN, Ahmad, "The Classical Definition of Qiyas in Islamic Jurisprudence", (1980) 19 *Islamic Studies* 23.

HAYDER, 'Ali, *Durar al-Hakkam,* a commentary on the Majalla, 4 volumes, Baghdad (nd), English trans. of the Majalla by C. R. TYSON, D. G. DIMITRIADES, and Ismail Haggi Effendi, Nicosia, 1901.

HICKS, S. C., "The Fuqaha and Islamic Law" 1978. A. J. C. L. Supple. 11.

HIDAYATULLAH, M., "The Role of the Qur'an in the Development of the Shariah" (1975) 6 *Islam and the Modern Age,* 57.

HILL, E, "Orientalism and Liberal-Legalism: the study of Islamic Law in the Modern Middle East", (1976) R. M. E. S. 57.

HOURINI, G. F., "The basis of Authority of Consensus in Sunnite Islam", (1964) 21 Studia Islamica 13.

HUGHES, T. P., *A Dictionary of Islam,* London, 1885.

HUMPHREYS, R. Stephen, Islam and Political Values in Saudi Arabia, Egypt and Syria, 33 *Middle East Journal,* 1979 pp. 1-19.

132

HURGRONJE, S., *Selected Works,* (tr. G. H. Bousquet and J. Schacht), Leiden, 1957.

IBN QUDAMA, Muwaffaq al-Din, *Al-Umda fi fiqh ibn Hanbal,* Damascus (nd), French translation by H. Laoust, *Le precis de droit d'ibn Qudama,* Beirut, 1950.

IBRAHIM, A., *Islamic Law in Malaya,* Singapore, 1965.

IQBAL, Sir Muhammed, *The reconstruction of Religious Thought in Islam,* Oxford, 1934.

ISHAQ, M., "Historical Survey of Fiqh and Muslim Jurisprudence", (1963), 8 J. A. S. Pakistan 27.

JAH, U., "The Importance of Ijtibad in the Development of Islamic Law" (1977) 7 J. I. C. L. 31.

JAIN, M. P., *Outlines of Indian Legal History,* Bombay, 3rd edition, 1972.

JONES, W., (editor Rumsey), *Al-Sirajiyyah* translated, Calcutta, 1890.

JUYNBOLL, Th. W., *Akila* in *Encyclopedia of Islam,* Leiden and London 1913-1934.

KERR, M. H., *Islamic Reform: Political and Legal Theories of Abduh,* 1967.

KHADDURI, Majid, *War and peace in the Law of Islam,* Baltimore, 1960.

KHADDURI, Majid, *Islamic Jurisprudence: Shafi'i's Risala,* Baltimore, 1961.

KHADDURI, Majid, *The Islamic law of Nations,* Baltimore, 1966.

KHADDURI, Majid, *The Islamic Concept of Justice,* Baltimore and London, 1984.

KHADDURI, Majid, "Property: Its relation to equality and freedom in accordance with Islam", in, *Equality and Freedom* (edited for the international Association of the Philosophy of law and Social Philosophy of Law and Social Philosophy), Wiesbaden, 1978.

KHADDURI, Majid, "nature and Sources of Islamic law", (1953) 20 Geo. W. L. R. 3.

KHADDURI, Majid and LIEBESNY, Herbert, *Law in the Middle East,* Washington D. C.: The Middle East Institute, 1955.

KHALID, S. R. *Muslim Law,* Lucknow, 2nd. edition, 1979.

KHALIL, S., *Ash-Shafi'i's Risalah: Basic Ideas,* 1974, Pakistan.

KHAN, W., "The Sunni Jurists and Principles of Legislation" (1960) 7 Justita 51.

KHAN BAHADUR, M. Y., "Mohammedan law" (Tagore Law Lectures 1891-1892), Calcutta, 1895.

KHOMEINI, Ruh-Allah, Islam and Revolution. (translated by H. Algar), Berkeley, 1981.

KREMER, V., *History of Islamic Civilisation.* (tr. Dhuda Buksh), Calcutta, 1905.

KRUSEM, Hans, The Islamic Doctrine of International Treaties, 1 *The Islamic Quarterly,* 1954, pp. 152-158.

LAMMENS, H., *Islam: Briefs and Institutions* (tr. Sir E. Denison Ross), London, 1929.

LATIFI, D., "Rationalism and Muslim Law", (1973) 4 *Islam and the Modern* Age 43.

LAYISH, A., *Women and Islamic Law in the Non-Muslim State,* New York, 1975.

LERRICK, Alison and MIAN, Q. Javad., *Saudi Business and Labour law: Its Interpretation and Application,* London, 1982.

LEVY, R., *The Social Structure of Islam,* Cambridge, 1957.

LEWIS, B., *The Arabs in History,* London, 1958.

LIEBESNY, Herbert, J., *The Law of the Near and Middle East: Readings, Cases and Materials,* Albany, New York 1975.

LING, T. C., "Islam's alternative to Fundamentalism" *Bulletin of the John Rylands U. L. of Manchester,* Volume 64 No. 1. 1981, 165.

MACDONALD, D. B., *Development of the Muslim Theology, Jurisprudence and*

Constitutional Theory, London, 1903, reprinted Lahore, 1964.

MACDONALD, D. B., *'Dar al-Harb'* in *Encyclopedia of Islam,* Leiden and London, 1913-1934.

MACNAUGHTEN, W. H., Principles and Precedents of Mohummudan Law, Calcutta, 1825.

MAHMASSANI, Subhi, *The Philosophy of Jurisprudence in Islam* being a translation of *Falsafat al-Tashari fi al-Islam,* by Farhat Ziadeh, (translator), Leiden, 1961.

MAHMOOD, Tahir, *Islamic Law in Modern India,* Bombay, 1972.

MAHMOOD, Tahir, "Custom as a source of Law in Islam" 1972. 14 J. I. I. L. 583.

MAHMOOD, Tahir, *The Muslim of India,* New Delhi, 1980.

MAHMOOD, Tahir, *Principles and Digest of Muslim Law,* Lahore, 1967.

MAHMOOD, Tahir, "Personal Laws of Bangladesh a Comparative Perspective", (1972) 14 J. I. L. I. 583.

MAHMOOD, Tahir, Muslim Personal Law: Role of the State in the Sub-Continent, New Delhi, 1977.

MAKDISI, G., "The Significance of the Sunni Schools of Law in Islamic Religious History," (1979) 10 I. J. M. E. S. 1.

MANNAN, M. A., *The Superior Courts of Pakistan,* Lahore, 1973.

MARGOLIOUTH, D. S., *Early Development of Mohamadanism,* London, 1914.

MAUDUDI, M., *Islamic Law and Constitution,* Lahore, 1967.

MERCHANT, M. V., *Qur'anic Laws,* Lahore 1947.

MORAND, M., *Avant-project de code presente a la Commission de Codification du droit musulman,* Algiers, 1916.

MORAND, M., *Etudes de droit musulman algerian,* Algiers, 1910.

MORAND, M., *Etudes de droit musulman. Les personnes morales en droit musulman,* Algiers, 1931.

MASUD, Muhammad Khabid, *Islamic Legal Philosophy,* Islamabad, 1977.

MUIR, William, *The Caliphate,: Its Rise, Decline and Fall,* London, 1891.

MUJEEB, M., "Orthodoxy and the Orthodox: The Shariah as Law", (1964) I.C. 27.

MULIA, Sir D. F., *Principles of Muhammaden Law.,* 15th edition, 1963.

MULIA, Sir D. F., *Sahih Muslim,* English translation by Abdul Hamid Addiqi, 4 volumes Lahore, 1976.

MULIA, Sir D. F., Principles of Mahomedan Law, Bombay 1976, (18th edition).

MISTRA, B. B., *The Central Administration of the East India Company,* Manchester 1959.

MUSTRA, B. B., *The Judicial Administration of the East India Company in Bengal 1765-1782,* Delhi, 1961.

NAFA, M. A., *Libyan Company and Business Law,* London, 1976.

NAQAVI, Sayid Ali Riza, *Family Laws of Iran,* Islamabad: Islamic Research Institute, 1971.

NAWAWI, Muhi al-Din Abu Zakariyya Yahya ibn Sharif, *Minhij al-Talibin:* Arabic text with French translation by L. W. C. Van Den Berg, Batavia 1804; English translation by E. G. Howard, London 1914.

NAWAZ, M. K., "A re-examination of some basic concepts of Islamic Law and Jurisprudence", (1963) 12 I. Y. B. I. A. 205.

NAWAZ, M. K., "Some aspects of Interpretation of Islamic Law in India in the past", (1960-1961), 10 I. Y. B. I. A. 127.

NELSON, B. N. *The Idea of Usury,* Princeton, 1949.

NIELSON, Jurgen S. "Mazalim and Dar al-Adl under the Early Mamluks.", *The Muslim World,* Volume LXV1, number 21, 1976.

NOORI, Yahya, *Islamic Government and the Revolution in Iran,* Glasgow, Royston Limited, 1984.

NOORI, Yayha, *Finality of Prophethood: An analysis of Babism and Baha'ism,* Tehran, 1981.

NOUR, A. M., "Qias as a source of Islamic law", (1974) 5 J. I. C. L. 18.

O'LEARY, (De Lacy Evans), *Arabia before Muhammad,* London, 1927.

PATRA, A. C., *The Administration of Justice under the East India Company in Bengal, Bihar and Orissa,* London, 1962.

PEARL. D. S., "A Historic Background to the Personal Systems of Law", (1974) *Studies in Islam* 95.

PEARL, D. S., "Interpersonal Conflict of laws between two classes", (1978) *India Socio-legal Journal,* Volume 4, Number 1.

PEARL, D. S., *Interpersonal Conflict of Laws: India, Pakistan and Bangladesh,* Bombay, 1981.

PEARL, D. S., *A Textbook on Muslim Law,* London, 1979.

PEARL, D. S., "Family Law in Pakistan" (1969) 9 Journal of Family Law.

PEARL, D. S., "The Legal Rights of Muslim Women in India, Pakistan and Bangladesh", (1976), 6 *New Community* 68.

PISCATORY, James Paul, *Islam and the International Legal Order: The Case of Saudi Arabia,* Dissertation, University of Virginia, May 1976.

POLIAK, A. N., "Classification of lands in the Islamic Law, and its technical terms, in the *American Journal of Semitic Languages and Literature,* (1940) pp. 50-62.

QADRI, A. A., *Islamic Jurisprudence in the Modern World,* Lahore, 1973.

QUERRY, A., *Recueil de lois concenant les musulmans schyites,* Paris, 1881.

RABBO, S. A., "Sources of Islamic Law", (1980) *The Search* 280.

RABIE, H., *The Financial System of Egypt 764-741 A. H./1160-1341 A. D.,* London, 1972.

RAHIM, A., *The Principles of Muhammadan Jurisprudence,* Madras, 1911.

RAHMAN, F., "Concepts Sunnah and Hadith in the Early Period", (1962) 1 *Islamic Studies* No. 1, 1.

RAHMAN, F., "Towards Reformulating and Methology of Islamic Law", (1979) 12 N. Y. U. J. of Int. Law and Politics 219.

RAMADEN, S., *Islamic Law: its Scope and Equity,* London, 1970.

RANKIN, C., "Custom in the Personal Law of India" (1939) 25 *Transactions of the Grotius Society,* 89.

RANKIN, C., *Background to Indian Law,* Cambridge, 1946.

ROBERTS, R., *The Social Laws of the Koran: Considered and Compared with those of the Hebrew and other Ancient Codes,* London, 1925 (reprinted 1971).

RUSSELL, A. D., and SUHRAWARDY, A. A. M., *First Steps in Muslim Jurisprudence,* 1963.

RYAN, M., *Health Services in the Middle East,* London, 1984.

RUXTON, F. H., *Maliki Law,* translation of the Mukhtasar of Sidi Khalil, London, 1916.

SAKSEAN, K. P. *"Muslim Law as Administered in India and Pakistan",* Lucknow, 1963 (4th edition).

DE SATILLA, David, Law and Society, in *The Legacy of Islam,* Oxford, 1931.

SCHACHT, Joseph, *The Origins of Muhammadan Jurisprudence,* Oxford 1953, (2nd edition).

SCHACHT, Joseph, *An Introduction to Islamic Law,* Oxford, 1964.

SCHACHT, Joseph, "Foreign Elements in Ancient Islamic Law", 32 *Journal of Comparative Legislation,* 1950 pp. 9-16.

SEAMAN, Bryant W., "Islamic Law and Modern Government: Saudi Arabia

Supplements the Shari'a to Regulate Developments", 18 *Columbia Journal of Transnational Law,* 1980 pp. 413-481.

SERVIER, A., *Islam and the Psychology of the Mussalman,* London, 1924.

SETALVAD, M. C., *The Common Law in India,* Cambridge, 1946.

SETALVAD, M. C. *The Role of English Law in India,* Jerusalem 1966.

SIDDIQI, M. Z., "The Importance of hadith as a Source of Islamic Law" 1964, *Studies in Islam,* 19.

SIRCAR, S. C., *The Muhammadan Law,* Tagore Law Lectures 1873, Calcutta 1873.

STRIVASTAVA, R. C., *Development of the Judicial System in India under the East India Company 1833-1858,* Bombay, 1971.

TANDON, M. P., *Text-Book of Mahomedan Law,* Allahabad, 1977.

TANZIL-wr-Ralman, *A code of Muslim Personal Law,* (two volumes Karachi 1978, 1980).

TREVELYAN, E. J., *The Constitution and Jurisdiction of Courts of Civil Justice in British India,* Calcutta, 1923.

TYABJI, F. B., *Muslim Law: The Personal Law of Muslims in India and Pakistan,* Bombay, 1968.

VERMA, B. R., *Mohammedan Law in India and Pakistan,* Delhi, 1978. 1978.

VESEY FITZGERALD, S., *Muhammadan Law,* London 1931.

VESEY FITZGERALD, S., "Muhammadan Law: An Abridgement according to its Various Schools", London, 1931.

WAKIN, J. (ed), *Function of Document in Islamic Law,* 1974.

WATT, M. M., *Islam and the Integration of Society,* London, 1961.

WATT, M. M., *Muhammad at Medina,* Oxford, 1956.

WEIR, T. H., "Diya" in Encyclopedia of Islam" Leiden and London, 1913-1934.

WEISS, B., "Interpretation of Islamic Law" (1978) 26 A. J. C. L. 199.

WENSINCK, A. J., *"Niya",* Encyclopedia of Islam, Leiden and London, 1913-1934.

WILSON, Ronald K., *Anglo-Muhammadan Law,* 6th edition, London, 1930.

WILSON, Ronald K., *Anglo-Muhammadan Law,* 6th edition, Calcutta, 1930.

YADUVANSH, U., "The Decline of the Role of the Qadis in India 1793-1876", (1969) 6 *Studies in Islam* 155.

YUSUF, S. M., "The Sunnah-its Transmission, Development and Revision", (1963) 37 I. C. 271.

ZAGDAY, M. I. Modern Trends in Islamic Law in *Current Legal problems,* London, 1948.

ZAIN AL-ABIDIN, Al-Tayyib, "The Yemeni Constitution and its Religious Orientation", 3 *Arabian Studies,* 1976, pp. 115-135.

ZIADEH, Farhat Joseph, *Property Law in the Arab World,* London, 1979.

2. Bibliography on South Yemen

AL-ABDALI, Ahmad Fadl bin Muhsin, *Hadiyyat al-Zaman fi Akhbar Muluk Lahij wa Adan* (Gift of the time on the history of the Kings of Lahij and Aden), Cairo: Salafiya Press, 1932.

AMNESTY INTERNATIONAL, *Briefing on People's Democratic Republic of Yemen,* London: Amnesty International, 1976.

BELL, Gawain, "A constitution for South Arabia", 55 *Royal Central Asian Journal* (Oct. 1966), pp. 266-76.

BIDWELL, Robin, *The Two Yemens,* London: Longman, 1983.

BRINTON, J. Y., *Aden and the Federation of South Arabia,* Washington D. C. American Society of International Law, 1964.

BUJRA, Abdallah, *The Politics of Stratification: Political Change in a South Arabian Town,* Oxford: Oxford University Press, 1971.

COUNTRYMAN, John R., South Yemen: the Socialist facade crumbles, *Middle East International,* 7 February 1986, pp. 11-13.

HAMILTON, R. A. B., *The Social Organisation of the Tribes of Aden Protectorate,* JRCAS, 1942.

GHANEM, Islam, *Social Aspects of the Legal Systems in South-West Arabia,* London, 1967.

GHANEM, Islam, "A note on Law No. 1 of 1974 concerning the family, People's Democratic Republic of Yemen" 3 *Arabian Studies* (1976), pp. 191-96.

GHANEM, Islam, *Yemen: Political History, Social Structure and Legal System,* London: Arthur Probsthain, 1981.

AL-HABASHI, Muhammad, *Political, Economic & Social Evaluation of South Arabia,* Algiers: Societs Nationale d'Edition et de Diffusion, 1966.

HALLIDAY, Fred, *Arabia Without Sultan,* New York: Vintage, 1975.

HASAN, Mohamed Salamen, *Report to the People's Republic of Southern Yemen on Guidelines for Industrial Planning and Policy,* United Nations, 1979.

HICKINBOTHAN, Sir Tom, *Aden, London: Constable, 1959.*

HUNTER, Frederick, *Account of the British Settlement of Aden in Arabia,* London: Frank Cass, 1968.

IBN HAJAR, of South Arabia, *Tuhfat al Muhtaj* (A commenatary on the *Minhaj al-Talibin* of Imam Nawawi), Calcutta, 1914.

INGRAMS, Doreen, *A Survey of the Social and Economic Conditions of the Aden Protectorate,* London, 1949.

JOHNSTON, Charles, *View from Steamer Point,* London: Collins, 1964.

KING, Gillian, *Imperial Outpost-Aden,* New York, Oxford University Press, 1964.

KNOX-MAWER, R., *Law Reports of Aden containing Cases determined by the Supreme Court of the Colony of Aden, 1937-53,* Aden, 1954.

KNOX-MAWER, R., "Islamic domestic law in the Colony of Aden", 5 *International and Comparative Law Quarterly* (1956), 511.

KOUR, A. H., *The History of Aden, 1839-1872,* London: Frank Cass, 1980.

LITTLE, Tom, *South Arabia: Area of Conflict,* London: Pall Mall Press, 1968.

McCLINTOCK, David, *The People's Democratic Republic of Yemen,* London, 1982.

MABGAR, A., al-Jihaz al-Qanuni ...(The legal system for an independent Southern Arabia), *Dirasat* (the organ of graduates' Congress), Aden, 3rd issue, April 1966, pp. 5-8.

MAKARI, A. M. A., *Water Rights and Irrigation practice in Lahij,* Cambridge: Cambridge University Press, 1971.

MAKTOUF, Lotfi, "Euro-Arab Arbitration Rules", 2 *Middle East Executive Reports* (1983), pp. 15-17.

MAWER, June Knox, *The sultana Came to Tea,* London: Murray, 1961.

MEKKAW, Al of Aden, Abdul Qadir, *al-nahr al-nahr an-fa'id* (The Overflowing River) Arabic text and English translation, printed in Aden, without date (but Text and German translation by Leipsic Hirsch, 1981).

MOLYNEUX, Maxine D., "State Policy and the Position of women in South Yemen", *People's Mediterraneans,* no. 12, July-September 1980, pp. 33-49.

NOORI, Y., et al, *Legal and Political Structure of an Islamic State,* Glasgow, 1986.

PAGET, Julian, *Last Post-Aden 1964-1967,* London: Faber and Faber, 1969.

PALGRAVE, *Central and Eastern Arabia,* 3rd Edition, 1866 (2 vols).

People's Democratic Republic of Yemen, A *Review of Economic and Social Development,* Washington D. C. World Bank, 1979.

People's Democratic Republic of Yemen (Ministry of Culture and guidance), *Why Nationalisation* (and Law No. 37 and 1969), Aden, 1970;

People's Democratic Republic of Yemen (Ministry of Culture and guidance), *Programme of the Unified Political Organisation, the National Front, for the National Democratic Phase of the Revolution,* London: PDRY Embassy, 1977.

PRIDHAM, B. R., *Economy, Society and Culture in Contemporary Yemen,* London: Croom Helm, 1985.

SERGEANT, Robert B., "Two tribal law cases in South West Arabia", JRAS, April, 1951, pp.33-47.

STOOKEY, Robert W, *South Yemen,* London: Croom Helm, 1982.

TREVASKIS, Sir Kennedy, *Shades of Amber, A South Arabian Episode,* London: Hutchinson, 1967.

UBAID, M., *Country Report on People's Democratic Republic of Yemen for feasibility study on management of the major regional aquifers in north-east Africa and the Arabian Peninsula,* Doha (Qatar), 1976.

UNITED KINGDOM (Colonial Office), *Accession of Aden to the Federation* of South Arabia, CMd. 1814, 1952;

UNITED KINGDOM (Colonial Office), *Ordinates enacted during the year 1946,* Aden: Government of the Colony of Aden, 1946;

UNITED KINGDOM (Colonial Office), *Aden and Yemen,* London: H.M.S.O., 1960;

UNITED KINGDOM, *Conference on Constitutional Problems of South Arabia,* London: H.M.S.O., 1961;

UNITED KINGDOM, *H.M's Order in Council Acts of Parliament, Proclamations and Subsidiary legislation published* in the Colony (of Aden) during the year 1946, Aden: The Government of the Colony of Aden, 1946;

UNITED KINGDOM, *Law Reports of Aden 1937-1951,* Aden: Government Press, 1954;

UNITED KINGDOM, *Qat Commission of Inquiry Report,* Aden, 1958;

UNITED KINGDOM, (Central Office of Information), Aden and South Arabia, London: H.M.S,O., 1965.

UNITED KINGDOM, *Proceedings of the Legislative Council,* 1941-67, Aden Government, 1967.

UNITED KINGDOM, Memorandum of Agreed Points relating to Independence of South Arabia (Geneva, 29 November 1967), London: H.M.S.O., Cmnd. 3504.

UNITED KINGDOM (Naval Intelligence Division), *Western Arabia and the Red Sea,* London, 1946.

VAN DER MEULEN, Daniel, *Hadramut, Some of its Mysteries Unveiled,* Leiden, 1932, reprinted 1964.

WATERFIELD, Gordon, *Sultans of Aden,* London: Murray, 1968.

WORLD BANK, *PDRY: A Review of Economic and Social Development,* Washington DC, 1979.

WORLD BANK, *PDRY: Mid-Term Review of Second Five Year Plan (1981-85),* Washington DC, 1983.

WORLD BANK, *PDRY: Appraisal Report on Health Development Project, 1982-87,* Washington DC, 1982.

ZABARAH, Mohammed Ahmed, *Yemen: Traditional Vs Modernity*, New York: Praeger, 1982.

3. Bibliography on North Yemen

AL-AKHRAS, H., *A Note on Land Tenure in Yemen*, San'a: Central Planning Organisation, 1972.

AL-ATTAR, *Le Yemen*, Paris, 1965.

ABU ZAHRA, Muhammad, *Tarikh al-Madhahib al-Islamiyya*, 2 volumes, Cairo (nd).

AL-HAMYI, Hussain ibn Ahmud al-Siba'i, *Al-Rawd al-Nadr Sharh Majmu al-Fiqh al Kabir*, 3 volumes, Cairo, 1921.

AL-QASIM, (ibn Muftah), Abdullah ibn Abi, *Sharh al-Azhar*, volume 2, Cairo (nd).

AL-SHAWKANI, Muhammad ibn 'Ali *Navl al-Awater*, 8 volumes, Cairo, 1938.

AMIN, S. H., *Marine Pollution in International and Middle Eastern Law*, Glasgow: Royston, 1986.

AMIN, S. H., *Law and Government in the Arab World*, Glasgow: Royston, 1986.

AMIN, S. H., *Middle East Legal Systems*, Glasgow: Royston, 1984.

AMIN, S. H., *Islamic Law in the Contemporary World: Introduction, Glossary and Bibliography*, Glasgow: Royston, 1985.

BOALS. Kathryn, Modernisation and Intervention: Yemen as a Theoretical Case Study, Ph.D. thesis, Princeton, 1970.

CHELHOD, Joseph, *Le droit dans la société bedouine*, Paris: Marcel Riviere et Cie, 1971.

CHELHOD, Joseph, *La société Yemenite et le droit*, 2 *L'Homme*, 1975, 67-86.

CHELHOD, J., Joseph, "La parenté et le mariage au Yémen." *L'Ethnographie* 67; 47-90.

CHELHOD, Joseph, "Les cérémonies du mariage au Yémen." *Objets at Mondes* 13 (1):3-14.

CHELHOD, Joseph, "Knives and Sheaths: Notes on a Sexual Idiom of Social Inequality in North Yemen." *Ethnos* 45: 82-91.

GERHOLM, T. *1977 Market, Mosque, and Mafraj: Social Inequality in a Yemeni Town*. Stockholm: Stockholm Studies in Social Anthropology.

GHANEM, I., *Social Aspects of the Legal Systems in South-West Arabia with special reference to the application of Islamic Law in the Aden Courts*, M. Phil. thesis, SOAS, 1973.

GHANEM, I., "Social Life in the Yemens and the role of tribal law", *Middle East International*, December 1972.

GHANEM, I., *Yemens: Political History, Social Structure and Legal System*, London: Arthur Probsthain, 1981.

AL-HADDAD, A. R., *Cultural Policy in the Arab Yemen Republic*, Paris: UNESCO, 1982.

HEYWORTH-DUNNE, G. E., *Al-Yemen: Social, Political and Economic Survey*, Cairo: Renaissance, 1952.

INGRAMS, Harold, *The Yemen: Imams, Rulers and Revolutions*, London, 1963.

JENNER, Michael, *Yemen Rediscovered*, London, Longman, 1983.

MACRO, Eric, *Bibliography of the Yemen, with notes on Mocha*, University of Miami Press, 1959.

MAKHLOUF. Carla, *Changing Veils: A Study of Women in North Yemen*, London Croom Helm, 1972.

MESSICK, B., "Transactions in Ibb: Economy and Society in a Yemeni Highland Town." Ph.D. dissertation, Princeton University, Princeton, N.J.

MUNDY, M., "Women's Inheritance of Land in Highland Yemen." *Arabian Studies,* vol. 5 (1978), pp.161-87.

MUSALLAM, Basim, *Sex and Society in Islam: Birth Control before the nineteenth Century,* (Cambridge Studies in Islamic Civilisation), 1984.

NOORI, Y., *Islamic Government,* Glasgow: Royston, 1985.

PETERSON, J. E., *Yemen, the Search for a Modern State,* London: Croom Helm, 1981.

PRIDHAM, Brian, ed., *Contemporary Yemen: Politics and Historical Development,* London: Croom Helm, 1984.

PRIDHAM, Brian, ed., *Economy, Society and Culture in Contemporary Yemen,* London: Croom Helm, 1984.

ROUAUDI, Alain, *Le Yemen,* Brussels, Editions Complexe, 1979.

SMITH, Rex, *The Yemens,* Clio Press, 1983.

STOOKEY, Robert, *Yemen: The Politics of the North Yemen Republic,* Boulder, Colorado: Westview Press, 1978.

TRITTON, A.S., *The Rise of the Imams of San'a,* London, 1928.

TUTWILER, R., "General Survey of Social Economic, and Administrative Conditions in Mahweet Province, Yemen Arab Republic." Final Report of Grant no. AID/NE-G-1308. Mimeograph in files of Agency for International Development, Sana.

UNITED KINGDOM: Colonial Office, *Aden and Yemen.* London, HMSO, 1960.

UNITED NATIONS, *Tax* Structure, government savings and tax problems: A case study of the Y.A.R., Beirut: U.N. Office, 1972.

WENNER, Manfred W., *Yemen: A Selected Bibliography of Literature since 1960,* Washington DC, Library of Congress Legislative Reference Services, 1965.

YEMEN ARAB REPUBLIC, al-Jaridah al-Rasmijah (Official Gazette), Sana, various volumes.

YEMEN ARAB REPUBLIC, The Constitution of 1962, in PEASLEE, A , *Constitutions of Nations,* revised 3rd edition.

YEMEN ARAB REPUBLIC, The Constitution of 1972, *The Official Gazette,* 30 December 1970 (English translation in 25 *Middle East Journal* (1971), pp. 389-401).

YEMEN ARAB REPUBLIC, *Ministry of Education Report,* 1965-66, Sanra, 1966.

YEMEN ARAB REPUBLIC, *Report on the 20th Anniversary of the September 1962 Revolution – the Banking Sector,* San'a, 1982.

YEMEN ARAB REPUBLIC, Central Bank, *The Financial Bulletin,* San'a, 1983.

YEMEN ARAB REPUBLIC, Ministry of Planning, *Second Five Year Plan (1981-86),* San'a, 1981.

YEMEN ARAB REPUBLIC, Ministry of Health, *Annual Report of Supreme Drug Board,* San'a, 1983.

ZAID, b. Ali, *Corpus Juris* (majmu'a *al-fiqh*) Arabic text edited by E. Griffeni, Milan, 1919.

ZABARAH, M. A., Yemen, *Traditionalism Vs Modernity,* New York: Praeger, 1982.

ZEIN AL-ABDIN, Al-Tayyib, "The Yemen Constitution and its Religious Orientation" 3 *Arabian Studies* (1976), pp. 115-135.

ZEIN AL-ABDDIN, Al-Tayyib, *The Role of Islam in the State, Yemen Arab Republic (1940-1972),* Ph.D. thesis, Fitzwilliam College, Cambridge, 1975.

About the Author

"Professor Doctor Amin ranks among the world's most distinguished authorities on Iranian and Islamic law and he is a prolific writer on these subjects, a number of which have been reviewed in our pages in recent times".

The Book Exchange: The international journal appraising new books in English, London, February, 1987.

"Dr. Amin displayed considerable courage in undertaking the description of the tangled skein of legal issues surrounding the conflicting claims to territory and access to maritime economic resources in the Gulf. Through th efforts of legal scholars like Dr. Amin, it is hoped that international process in the Gulf can be conducted by means of the peaceful arts of diplomacy, arbitration and negotiation".

Marshall W. Wiley, former U.S. Ambassador to Oman, American Arab Affairs, 1983, pp. 112--1113.

"Sayed Hassan Amin, born in Iran and practising law in London, is well-known abroad as an authority on Islamic law. This latest work certainly supports his reputation".

Professor Eve Evans, School of Law, New York University, *Journal of International Law and Politics,* Spring 1986.

"Amin, an international lawyer, is at his best in covering the legal aspects of Gulf security".

Professor John C. Campbell, *Foreign Affairs,* Winter 1984, p. 426-428.

"As an academic jurist, Dr. Amin is at his best on constitutions, marine law, the *Shari'a* and human rights. He is familiar with text and documentations. His heart is in the right place. He is in favour of democracy and the rule of law, which he honestly does not find in the Middle East. He recommends regional co-ordination, economic development by appropriate technology, "Marshall aid" from the Gulf Co-operation Council to make good the damage of the war between Iran and Iraq and "political, social and cultural progress" without too much Westernisation.
Dr. Amin tries hard to be objective in his analysis and even-handed between the combatants. But he had no sympathy for the Ba'ath regime of Iraq, "brutal" and "unpopular", noting on the other hand, that the Iranian revolution enjoyed the "near-total support of all social classes". Nevertheless, in a chapter devoted to the violation of human rights in Iran, he does not spare the appalling record of the Iranian revolutionaries, nor "mob-rule".

Professor A.R.H. Kellas, *Middle East International,* November 1984, pp. 18-19.

Samples of reviews concerning previous books by the same author

"For its opriginality, for the references it contains, and the enlightening accounts it conveys, *Middle East Legal Systems* seems to me an indispensable instrument of work for any person involved in Middle Eastern Affairs".

Nabil Saleh, *Muslim Education Quarterly*, 1986, pp. 91-93.

"The book is well written and produced with a comprehensive index. The material has been well researched and its bibliography will be useful to anyone wishing to gain more in depth information on any particular country or area of law. The book will be useful not only to students and academics with an interest in Middle East, but also to legal practitioners dealing with the complex problems involving the law of the Islamic countries of the Middle East".

Doreen Hinchcliffe, *The Arab Gulf Journal*, April 1986, pp. 87-88.

"An outstanding contribution on the legal systems of the Middle East countries by a leading authority in this field".

Hilmar Kruger, *Der Islam*, 1986, pp. 357-359

"Amin's book is a fine contribution to the study of the legal systems of fifteen Middle East countries that base their legal systems on Islam. As it stands, Middle East Legal Systems, is a thorough and expertly researched encyclopedia of many of the legal systems of the Islamic Middle East".

Eva Evans, *New York University Journal of International Law and Politics*, Spring, 1986, pp. 1057-58.

"*Middle East Legal Systems* and *Islamic Law in the Contemprorary World,* a possible companion to the first one, are essential to the international lawyer's library."

K. Khashayar, *American Journal of International Law*, 1986.

"The survey of Iran in particular is a comprehensive and wide-ranging study, while that of Iraq is also authoritative and informative."

R.B. Sargeant, *Asian Affairs*, June, 1986.

"providing a solid understanding of the law in this geographic region."

The George Washington Journal of International Law, 1985, pp. 629-630.

INDEX

Barley, 15
Bayhan (PDRY), 25, 27
Bedouins, 58
Bigamy, 65
Bills of Exchange Act 1941, 35
Birth, Death and Marriages
 Registration Act 1941, 34
Bombay (India), 25, 43
Books, monopoly on, 39
Bourgeosie, 29
Breast feeding, 67
Bridegrooms, 68, prospects of, 68,
 status of, 68
Brides, 67-68, fathers of, 68, guardians
 of, 68
British Advisors, 24
British Bank of the Middle East, 88
British Court of Appeal for Eastern
 Africa, 43
British Empire, *see* United Kingdom
British Nationality Act 1950 (UK), 34
British Petroleum (BP), 10
Brothers, 68
Building materials, import of, 39, for
 government projects, 39
Bureau of Ifta and Tashri' (YAR), 48

Cabinet (YAR), 47, 50, 57
Cables, 61
Canning factories, 41, administration
 of, 41, finance of, 41
 management of, 41
capital, 38, 88, external, 38
capital punishment, 36
Carriage of Goods by Sea Act 1941, 35
catha edulis, 64
cement, import of, 39
Census Act 1945, 34
Central Bank Law 1971 (YAR), 74
Central Bank of North Yemen (YAR),
 15, 74-77
Central Committee (PDRY), 31
Centralism, 10, 22, 30, 36, democratic,
 22, 30
Centralist economy, 10
Charitable and Religious Trusts Act
 1939, 35
Chief Magistrate's Court (PDRY), 43
Child Marriage Restraint Act 1939,
 35-36
Children, 36, 66, 69-72, 89,
 abandonment of, 72,
 acknowledgement of, 72,

affiliation of, 72, exploitation of, 36,
 illegitimate status of, 72 support of,
 69-72
China, 10-11
Christianity, 24, 67
Circular No 1 1980 (YAR), 64
Civil Code 1973-1979 (YAR), 56, 66
Civil Courts Act 1937, 34
Civil Courts of Appeal (PDRY), 43
Civil liberties, 29
Civil Procedure Code 1981 (YAR), 56
Civil War 1986 (PDRY), 11-12, 19, 22,
 26, 28-29, 87, 107, 109
Civil War (YAR), 48
Clans, 42
Classes, 22, 29, struggle between, 22,
 29
Coastlines, 40
Coersion, 62
Coffee, 15, 64
Cold stores, 41, administration of, 41,
 finance of, 41, management of, 41
Collectivisation, 10-11, 22, 29, 37, 102,
 of leadership, 22
College of Law (PDRY), 46
Colonial Office, *see* United Kingdom
Colonialism, 31-32
Commerce, 17, 56, 75, 78, 87
Commercial Code 1976 (YAR), 56
Communism, 30, 35-38, 110
Compensation, 37, 58
Confession, 59-60
 admissibility of, 59
 validity of, 59
Congress, Law Library of, 59
Constitution 1970 (PDRY), 29-30, 43
Constiturion 1978 (PDRY), 30, 35,
 37-38
Constitutional Amendment 1978
 (PDRY), 29
Constitutional Commission 1979
 (PDRY), 19
Constitutional Law, 29-30, 47-48,
 50-51, 54-56
Consultative Council (YAR), 47, 50-51,
 55-56, status of, 55
Consumer goods, 18
Continental margin, 40
Continental Shelf, 40, 115-123
 exploitation of resources of, 40
 outer limit of, 40
Contracts, 35, 37, 66-67, breach of, 35,
 conditional, 35, marriage, 37,

144

146

147

Internationalism, 86
Investment, 18-19, 38-39, 74, 87-88
  foreign, 38-39, 77, 87
  schemes for, 18
Investors, 38
Iran, 48, 53, 92, 95, 100, 103, 106-108
Iraq, 28, 41-42, 95, 100, 103
Islam, 8, 8(n), 14-15, 24, 26-28, 36,
  43, 48(n), 51, 53, 53(n), 54-57, 59(n),
  61, 64-68, 72-74, 77, 79-87, 90-96, 99,
  102-108, 110
  arbitration awards under, 27
  Batinite doctrines of, 53(n)
  belief, concealment of, 53
  Caliphs, 93, 95, 104
  family law of, 27
  Hadawi jurisprudence, 53, 85
  Hidden Imam, 53
  husbands' rights in, 36
  Imamites, 53(n), Imam, 24, 48(n),
  51, 53, 53(n), 77, 79, 85, 92-96,
  103-104, 106-108, 110
  Ishma'ilite school of, 53, 53(n),
  95-96, 103
  Ja'fari school of, 93, 106
  judgements in, 27
  legal traditions of, 50(n), 110,
  Methodological school of, 8(n)
  nass, 53-54
  penal code of, 26
  pre-Islamic customs, 27
  Shafi'i school of, 8, 8(n), 14, 28, 53,
  65, 99, 103
  Shi'a school of, 14, 24, 48, 51, 53,
  53(n), 92-95, 99, 103, 106
  Sunni schools of, 8, 8(n), 14, 51, 77,
  92-95, 99, 103, 106
  jurisprudence of, 53
  Twelvers, 53(n), 53, 92, 94-95
  Ulama, 27
Islamic Development Bank, 21
Islamic Law, 27-29, 31, 34-36, 43, 51,
  53, 56-58, 63, 65, 67, 72, 74, 79,
  84-87, 91-96, 103-105
Islamic State, 24
Isma'il, Abd al-Fattah (President of the
  (PDRY, 1978-1980), 12, 28
Ismail, Shi'a Imam, 53(n), 95
Israel, 39-40, 78
Ithna Ashari, 92-95

Japan, 41-42

Jerusalem (Israel), 24
Ja'far-as-Sadiq, Imam (d. 740 AD),
  53(n), 92-95
Jama'at-e Islami, 92
Jewellery, 68
Jordan, 48
  Judaism, 43, 67
Judgement, 48, 51
  enforcement of, 48
Judiciary, 31, 42-44, 46, 48, 51, 54,
  56-57, 59-61, 65, 72-73, 79-84, 86
  appointment of, 80, apprenticeship
  for, 46, authority of, 56, committee
  of (YAR), 57, discretion of, 60, dual
  system of, 43, freedom of, 61,
  functions of, 54, 79, independence
  of, 57, 79
Juries, 43, 59, 61
  absence of, 59
Jurisdiction, 44, 57, 60, 75, 80, 82
  civil, 44, criminal, 44, delimination
  of, 82
Justice, 44, 47-84
  administration of, 44
Kafa', 68
Kamaran (Island, YAR), 78
KFAED, 21
Khomeini, Ayatollah, 100
Kiswa, 68
Kosygin, Aleksei Nikolayevich (Prime
  Minister of the USSR), 12
Kufa (Iraq), 92
Kutama (Island, YAR), 78
Kuwait, 18, 20(n), 41, 56, 74, 85, 89,
  100

Lacuna, 57
Land, 37-38, 56, 77
  confiscation of, 37, ownership of, 77,
  tenure of, 38
Landlords, 37, 102
Langoustes, 42
Language, 20, 55, 63
Law (PDRY), 29-31, 34-38, 40-43, 46,
  91, 102
  administrative, 31, civil, 35,
  common, 31, 34, 37, 43,
  constitutional, 29-30, contract, 35,
  criminal, 35-36, 43, 102
  customary, 34, 36, 42-43
  economic, 37-40, family, 35-37, 91
  foreign investment, 38, industrial,
  35, of the sea, 40-42, private, 31,
  public, 31, schools of, 46, social, 37,

149

153

United Kingdom, 8, 10, 22, 24-29, 31-36, 42-44
Aden Colony Loan 1953, 34,
Aden Protectorate Levies 1939, 34
Aden Protectorate Rulers' State Troop 1940, 34
Admirality, legal affairs of, 43
Arbitration Ordinance 1941, 44
Authentification of Documents Act 1942, 34
Banking Act 1952, 35
Birth, Death and Marriages Registration Act 1941, 34
Carriages of Goods by Sea Act 1941, 35
Census Act 1945, 34
Charitable and Religious Trusts Act 1939, 35
Child Marriage Restraint Act 1939, 35-36
Civil Courts Act 1937, 34
Colonial Office, 25
Contracts Act 1938, 35
Court Registrar, 43
Defence White Paper 1966, 26
in India, 35, Middle East Command, 26, naval power of, 31-32, Order in Council 1944, 25, Privy Council, Judicial Committee of, 43
Protectorate Territories of, 24
rule of in Aden, 25-26, 29, 31, 35-36, 42, 44, withdrawal of from Aden, 10, 29, 35

UK-Federation of South Arabia Treaty, 27
United Nations, 10, 26, 42, 103
Special Committee on Decolonisation, 26
Universal Declaration of Human Rights 1948, 103
United Political Organisation National Front (UPONF) (PDRY), 30
United States of America, 12
Upper Aulaq (PDRY), 25, 27
Uqban (Island, UAR), 78
Urbanisation, 20, 31
Urf, 43, 51, 56, 110-113
Urmak (Island, YAR), 78
Usage, 43, 51, 56, 110-113
Usury, prohibition of, 74
Uthman (3rd Republican Caliph, d. 656 AD), 94

Vanguard Party (PDRY), 28, 30
Vendettas, 65
Vertical control, 30

Wage restraint, 15
War, 47, 65
declaration of, 47
Warrants, 60
Washington DC (USA), 59
Water, rights over, 56
Wealth, 68
Weapons, 61, 65
Wheat, 15
Witnesses, 59, 61-62, 66, 79
Wives, 36-37, 66-69, 73, 105
apostasy of, 73
conversion of to Islam, 73
duties of, 37
protection of, 69
representatives of, 66
rights of, 37
Women, 29, 31, 37-37, 61-62, 65, 67, 89, 104-106, discrimination against, 36, emancipation of, 36-37, organisations of, 31
Work ethic, 29
Workforce, 11, 29-31, 29, 102
organisations of, 31
remittances by, 11
World Bank, 21
Worship, places of, 55

Yaha, Imam, 19, 48
Yemen Arab Republic
administration, 47-48, power of, 47
Agricultural Credit Bank, 75
agriculture, 15, 17-18, 75
aid, external, 15, 18, 20
aircraft, 60
anti-imperialism, 27
appeals, 63, 79
courts of, 79
right of, 79
arbitration, 54, 56-57
armed forces, 47, 50, 54
role of, 54
balance of payments, 15, 17-18
banking, 57-58, 74, 101
banks, 74-76, 88
commercial, 75
specialised, 75-76
Bureau of Ifta and Tashri, 48
Cabinet, 47, 50, 57

YAR (continued)
Central Bank Law 1971, 74
Central Bank of North Yemen, 15,
74-77
Children, 66, 69-72, 89
abandonment of, 72
acknowledgement of, 72
affiliation of, 72
illegitimate, status of, 72
support of, 69-72
Circular No. 1 1980, 64
Civil Code 1973-1979, 56, 66
Civil Procedure code 1981, 56
Civil War, 48
commerce, 17, 56, 75, 78
Commercial Code 1976, 56
compensation, 58
Consultative Council, 47, 50-51,
55-56, status of, 55
contracts, 66-67
corporations, formation of, 48, 75
Council of Ministers, 47-48, 82
courts, 51, 54, 57, 59-63, 79-84
classification of, 80
constitution of, 80, 82-83
of appeal, 79-80
of first instance, 80
of summary jurisdiction, 80
organisation of, 79-83
preliminary, 80, 82
Shari'ah, 80-82
specialised, 82-83
traffic, 82
creation of, 50, 56
Criminal Procedure Code 1979, 56,
59-63
currency, 74, 77
Currency Board, 74
custom, 15, 51, 56, 58, 65-66, 68-69,
72, honour by, 58, legal system
based on, 56
debts, 56
Decree No. 15 1967, 78
Decree No. 16 1967, 78
development, 15, 18-21
political, 19-20
spending on, 15, 18, 21
disputes, 56
divorce, 65, 67, 73
domestic resources, 19
drugs, imports of, 78
economy, 15-21, 64, 75, 98, 108.
development of, 15, 19

mixed sector, 17, 75
planned, 17
private sector of, 17, 19, 75
public sector of, 17, 75
sectors of, 75
structure of, 15-21, 110
education, 18, 101
evidence, 54, 56, 59-61, law of, 54, 56
executive, 47-48, 50, 55, 79,
functions of, 54, 79
Executive Council, 50
exports, 57, 101
Familt Law 1978, 56, 65-67, 69,
72-73, 105
farmers, 75
farming, 75
fish, production of, 88
Five Year Development Plan
1977-1982, 18, 75
Five Year Development Plan
1982-1986, 18-19
foreign relations, 15, 20
Foreign Trade Company, 75
Gas, 17-18, 99
geography, 8, 14
government, 47-48, 50-51, 56
local, 48
national, 47
regional, 48
structure of, 50
gross domestic product, 15
Head of State, 47, 50, 55
High Council of Justice, 81-83
High Court of Appeal and Cassation,
63, 80-82, 84
Civil Chamber of, 81
Commercial Chamber of, 81,
deputies of, 80-81, Examination of
Court Decisions Chamber of, 81
General Assembly of, 81
jurisdiction of, 81
Personal Status Chamber of, 81
President of, 80-82
Housing, 75-76, 100
Housing Credit Bank, 75
husbands, 66-67, 72-73
apostasy of, 73
rights of, 73
illiteracy, 15, 89
imprisonment, 61, 63-64
independence, 48
industry, 17, 75, 88, 96
inheritance, 65, 72

158